Issue 4

INVERTED SYNTAX PRESS   November 2022

Inverted Syntax Print Issue 4 | November 2022

Inverted Syntax is an independently run art and literary magazine published annually in print and periodically online through the *Fissured Tongue* series. Starting in 2020, *Inverted Syntax* moved their print issue release from January to November, publishing two issues that year and none in 2021.

All included work is assumed to be original, with all written work assumed to be previously unpublished.

Print issues are published by *Inverted Syntax Press LLC,* P.O. Box 2044, Longmont, Colorado 80502. www.invertedsyntax.com

Print Issues are available at www.invertedsyntax.com.

Copyright © 2019–2022 *Inverted Syntax Press*
ISBN: 979-8-9872317-0-8
First Edition: November 2022

Issue 4 Volunteer Editorial Board
All staff members shared in the responsibility of reading and selecting work for Issue 4.
Editor Nawal Nader-French **Associate Editors** Jesica Davis, Allissa Hertz, Melanie Merle, Yesica Mirambeaux
Editorial Assistants Ginny Short, Miranda Martinez-Herbert
Additional Readers Ted Downum, Traci L. Jones, Jason Masino
Advisory Board Eric Baus, Traci L. Jones, Andrea Rexilius

2022 Fissured Tongue Series Managing Editor Yesica Mirambeaux

Front and back cover art *Quinta-VI—Character Art* by N'Dea Tucker, 3000 x 3000 pixels, digital art, 2022 (cropped)

Excerpt on back cover is from "*the landscape of the river*" by E. A. Midnight (page 88)

Submissions
We accept submissions only through our submission manager. Our general submission window is typically open February through June and the *Sublingua Prize for Poetry* submission window is typically open June through August. Should there be a Sublingua contest, the judge will be announced in spring 2023. As always, all poetry contest submissions will be read by the editorial staff, editors, and the judge, none of whom will have access to the identities of the submitters. The editors will meet as a group to select up to thirty semi-finalists to be sent to the judge, who will select finalists, one runner-up, and the winning poem, which will be awarded a monetary prize as well as the new **Sublingua Writing Retreat Prize**. The runner-up will be awarded the **Sublingua Writing Retreat Prize.**

[C O N T E N T S]

[Art]

◉

[2022 *Sublingua Prize for Poetry*]

Judged by *Inverted Syntax* Editorial Board

1st Prize Winner

ELISÁVET MAKRIDIS

Runner-up

JORDAN ANDERSON

Finalists

JORDAN ANDERSON   CARRIE VESTAL GILMAN

KS LACK   ROBERT OKAJI

◉

The Sublingua Prize Longlist

Editors selected poems submitted to the *Sublingua Prize for Poetry*
by the following writers for publication:

LISA BERLEY   SERENA RODRIGUEZ

ARIA PAHARI   YU HSUAN WU

INVERTED SYNTAX

Human expression is never orderly. It is a space of disruption. To let ourselves express means to be vulnerable. It means to invert syntax so as to articulate the visceral.

Quinta-VI—Character Art by **N'Dea Tucker,** 3000 x 3000 pixels, digital art, 2022

scavenger hunt

find a ship without legs
& then ride it to the hole in your sock.
we were talking about
driving eight hours to find the body.
your dorm room flood from the ceiling.
refuse to eat for days
in the hopes of transforming
into a butterfly. you would like
a break from daylight. find a night
that lasts as long as you need it to.
drilling holes in both hands
to feign stigmata. telling moths
they can fly through the openings.
find an envelope you never sent.
the post office covered in gold.
limited edition travels. the airplane
we took to visit desire. eating ice cream
in front of dinosaurs. your uncle
ran around with his hands on fire
& no one helped him put them out.
when i say you're searching i mean
i bought a shovel. go outside.
each darkness into the city streets
as if you're going to find a whale graveyard.
squirrel skull. owl pellet
with a vole heart still beating inside.
what terrifies you most is
not knowing what to look for.

maybe a comet. a celestial body. one to wear
when this one is done. find sleep.
find silverware. find a lover,
one who doesn't close their eyes like me.
who walks around like a search light.
i had that & we totaled your car
& the ship didn't have any legs
so we had to paddle on dry land.
find an ocean. toss your skull
into the water. listen to the crabs
as they play fiddles. the letter arrives without a stamp.
a car pulls away. find a citrus fruit
to serve as the sun. hang it
from the window. use crayons to
outline my body against
the bedroom wall. find a way
to save each touch. my hair
in an old jam jar. to keep is
to never have to hunt for again.
we have so so so many basements full.

Jordan Anderson

native girl (organic material, fabric)

the native girl in the museum as i am could not i think be understood

without description running long as my shadow does

under lowe's feather canoe, a light fixture.

"the artist standing in the exhibit with her mother or

a friend purses her lips as she says 'they.' 'they would

make these toy boats out of scraps' but then she wonders

who am i. if they are they just as white lady turns the corner

and points a white shed-snakeskin claw at 'they.'"

the native girl in the museum then wonders "why am i

here in this museum" where nothing can be said except for they

because i needs no museum where mirror suffices. even

this colonial ripple is discount where nestlé

takes water of they and sells it back to they i look up

would have been my culture online. "the artist

is an enthusiast which is to say her feet are severed cold and she is

quite meditative on walking, podiatrics."

the native man in the museum transgresses the glass

between i and they and i am in a locker room wondering

how they the others do it so effortlessly. my curse begins

with his long hair and bolo tie and ends with the pink beaded fringe

earrings which sit in my jewelry box at home like the bifurcated

tongue of an unteased oyster. "the artist wishes being native
meant she could approach this man and he'd see cousin
and not strange demilunatic in marc jacobs dress, silk, secondhand."

"the artist wishes she were more native than she is." "the artist
neglects to realize that having been taught nothing about either native
culture by either parent is one of the most native things
about her." "the artist regrets to mention earrings knowledge language
of hers are from online not passed down." "the artist acknowledges
genocide looping direct indirect knowledge weaving indistinguishable."
"the artist artifice and artifacts." "the artist is we we we and we all tumble
down the creek to send our scrap birch boats to wash, inevitable."

Beatrice Szymkowiak

Viscera
with words from J.J. Audubon's Birds of America (1827-38)

The abandoned sticks of hour cling
to claws. We wait until *farewell the orb*

devours our last / ing. Sunrise, again
sunset mingled in ploughed earth, yields

tubercles of rambling dusk. How hunger
hobbles the graceful notes / we feign

midsummer warble with bluish angle,
sing evergreens / ascending solitude.

Blades of Grass

with words from J.J. Audubon's Birds of America (1827-38)

Forgetful dancers bloom out
of their breasts / as if

they were brothers, perform
the impossible escape beyond

which / we found ourselves,
monsters of granite crumbling

down the morrows. There / we are
astonishment intermixed with grass,

gleaning among willows
for the beginning of March.

Of Be/coming

with words from J.J. Audubon's Birds of America (1827-38)

An eclipse now roosts beneath our wings.
We hear wolves howl & the monosyllables

of an axe. Trees are felled, then named.
We compose clocks with sticks, hang them

around our necks / forget the old elm,
that would gnarl wood into wishes. Maps

peel off from beech logs. We mask
with torn legends & act *l'orée du bois*

as a clearing. When fog moans through
the forest / a cage is lit to guide our path.

We vanish, deer blossom.

FRAME

1. : to construct   fit and unite   parts of the skeleton   (a structure)

2. : to contrive evidence   against (a person)   so a verdict of guilty   is assured

3. : physical makeup   of an animal   especially a human body

4. : one picture   on a length   of film

Jenny Grassl

DIARY OF DEER WOMAN

over a bed preened to swallow

living bodies of ghost-fit   a visit of catastrophes

I spread brown velvet

dredged   shined

my antlers reach too high for me to rest my head

I vanish with a hound

hunted imprints with hunter

phantom archers will tell you how sweet

among the succulents

                              to browse by night

my husband can't sleep here   the antlers disarrange him

              the screech of the howlers swinging from tine to tine

{ { { { { { { { { {

Body as Eschaton

Tree in lagoon,

                    body as eschaton:
                    a limit named epidermis,

the prolepsis of root.

Call it swamp, but the tree
has no root.

                    First remember the body's
                    places: the places *for* not *of*
                    the body you inhabit.
                    Both *place* and *reemerge*.

The surface of the water
admits no depth.

                    Body as clock: first forget
                    sleep and other absences
                    of the body from time. Remember
                    times of action in sequence
                    or in alternation. Times of *same*.

Sunshine.

                    Next delete etymology:
                    a whiteness of symbols.

Nearby stands an angular
stone complex. Dusk.
Squat tree.

The body reemerges
as its own horizon, its
own sex, its power. Body
as phoenix: exert the body.

Wind avoids this place.

Build the body: pulleys, a sock, wagon, wrench,
pushpins, microscope, shotgun,
a socket, pen, slippers, tape,
rope, needle, chain, gloves, mower,
rattle, fin, latch, cars, a ring,
nut, bat, phonograph, buckles,
snap, cleats, a vase, machete,
string, plates, bar, lever, doorbell.

People paddle toward the tree
mistaking it for somewhere.

How to hold another body,
its own sex, its power? Times
of *same*. Is there room
for relation? Hold the body.
There shall be time until *forget
its times*. Pose the body, your
own body.

The lagoon has swallowed cars
and [list of objects].
Flat water.

I understand your
body through its hold on mine. Own your
body, own it, immortal
body, but not its places.

Somewhere in Between by **Jane Williams**, 12 x 9 inches, Indian ink
on paper, 2019

i had a form

watch this moon ripple, its crater ribald perfection. play it like a drum,

like a hollow cheek—listen—a baritone choir carries a baby to almost—long

enough to rot this image, forgotten apple in a backseat. the summer months carry us

through from disgrace to mercy. ten years have passed since this city wasn't built with burn

scars running along the spine. i make bread when i'm lonely, when i let myself believe in control.

when my home fills with cinnamon, fills with tones of my grandmother—a southern voice soothing senses

into believing in all that is simple and good—i fall into childhood, a time before i knew how

failure tasted, how bravery aches and anger sticks fast to the bones. if i had a say, i would

spend afternoons running through slug-filled pastures. i would open jars and whisper

fly to lightning bugs wishing to be falling stars. and you would mimic dreams of

the little girl who just wanted her doll baby to be real and for drums to be an

instrument to play until your mind was quiet, your fingers blistered.

Complete Phase Cancellation

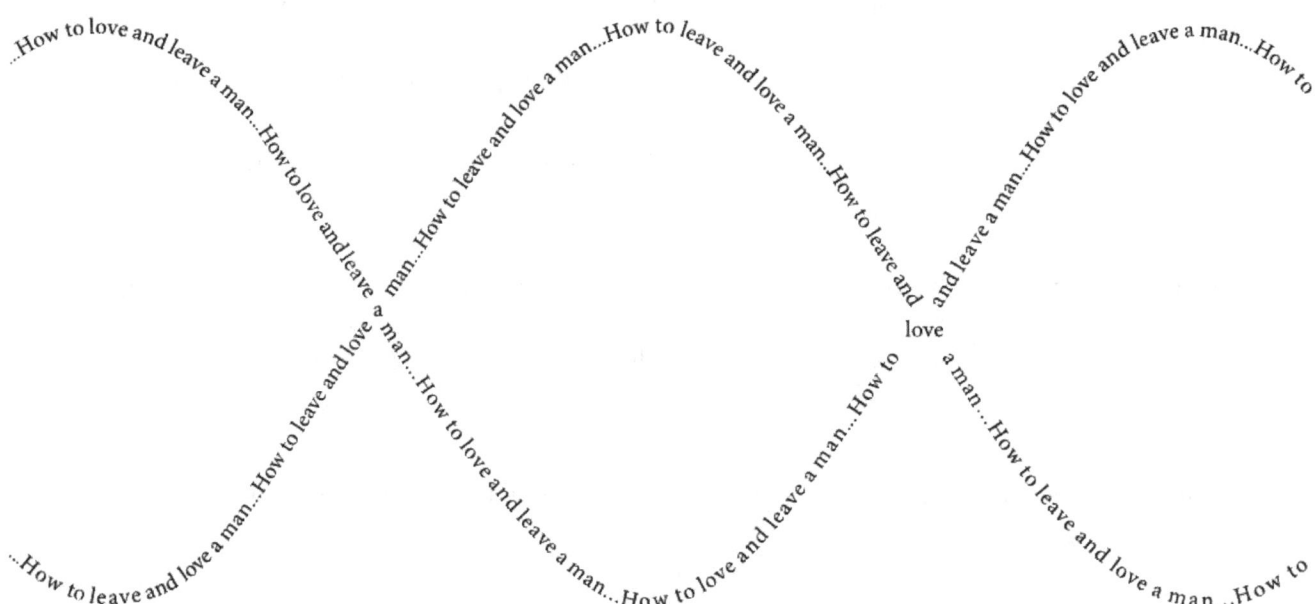

Compton Scattering

We are colliding light and electrons on a day like this one. We are interacting with cadmium and cesium. With metal rods and multiplier tubes with oscilloscopes. Our isotope is long-lived and its decay involves a single gamma ray. All this on a beautiful day. Such a beautiful collision. Look out the window. I remember you on a different day. You say the electron can be absorbed by a thin metal film or enough of an air path. You are saying this.

We love to think of light colliding with it does not matter what. There are as you insist many ways to arrange a sentence. This equation is an observation. There are two energies it insists. A before and after. A photon one way before. One way after and a scattering. The classical theory fails to account for this.

I want to shortcut to what is strange in this. To say I was there and remember the crystal scintillator. You ask what poet will furnish us with the metaphors for it. For which this new language cries out. Cries you say. An urgency in it. This observation that classical electromagnetism cannot account for.

$$E'_\gamma = \frac{E_\gamma}{1 + (\frac{E_\gamma}{m_e c^2})(1 - \cos\theta)}$$

You tell me the mood in the room has been scattered by aluminum and brass targets. There is warning in it. In my lab notebook the room is brass and moody and long-lived. You paraphrase as a function of the scattering angle. I draw our equipment do I faithfully copy the shadows. Are we showing that E=hν. Was I ever there in the present tense. Have I shortcut again.

I measure the angles and energies on a day like this one or this one. At 30 degrees I take data for five minutes live time. You say that time acts through repetition more than through duration. Later I will say that according to my lab report all of this occurred on a beautiful day.

Can you make meaning of this. Of large gray blocks and a shield.

Green in Prism

Boat-turn, my body angles toward the rippling surface, hand making contact. Not to sink underwater, but to be in that color. Lit emerald; sun-shot chlorophyll.

I make a room into a green lake catching light. I have an obsession with circumstance. With simulations.

The prison's interior spearmint walls resemble tiles of gum or new leaves. They induce dreams of pulling an ache through a tooth or a blossom from a branch.

A course in institutions, fluorescent lighting wreaks strange effects: a buzz of molecular restlessness, the body pacing just under the skin's surface, plus a hint of anesthesia.

Human constructions, strategic light: the galley, the gallery, the regal hall of mirrors. On the long corridor walls and on the library walls,

incarcerated artists have painted giants: men and women in uniform; a tractor in cornfields; the Maquoketa Caves; John Wayne's face; an industrial windmill. Memory is an outskirt where icons loom. Bend in the brain,

this loving refraction. This amplitude. Some weighted regret passes through all of us and breaks into colors, into saints and mountain faces. I sink bare feet in the neighbor's plush grass, insanely green. The world will turn your mind, it will make itself shine too plainly. Saints in the trees, chanting, spying. Out of the rock springs color, many-veined.

A jade plant, gangly and massive, sits in the corner, budding thumbs. I think of mood rings, of lagoons. I swim in one as I write. I rotate in my chair,

looking for the faces I know. Insiders and outsiders in the prison choir. They migrate around the gym to encircle the audience. Their path sings in rounds, gathering sorrows. They hum tree crowns, ancient, patina-ed bowls.

Untethered by **Jane Williams,** 12 x 12 inches, acrylic on board, 2019

VR brother

in game mode, we talk about girls.
he says he is waiting for perfect legs
& a jar of tongues.
really, i stand in the living room
knocking over glass vases.
shattering. meanwhile, in VR
i am just trying to hug him.
the headset sings a song about distances.
since he converted to digital
we have almost nothing
to say. i tell him it is raining
& he changes the sky to be purple &
heavy with clouds. he says, "what rain?"
this is not dreaming. this is
emptying each room on the front lawn.
i'm thinking about how we used to
talk through the dark
of our shared bedroom
as if night were a curtain.
him asking, "are you still awake?"
me pausing before whispering, "yes."
i ask him what he does all day
& he transforms his hand into a blue jay.
in VR, nothing is permanent
but especially not mistakes.
he runs away & returns. he chops down

a tree out of anger & instantly
it grows back. he says,
"don't you wish the rest of the world
was so forgiving?" a part of me does.
a part of me wants to burn
my house down & turn around
to see it back. but, then,
there are the pieces of a wreck.
how, even if they are ash,
they should be taken. held.
he shaves his head. he eats with his fingers.
tells me he is in love with
a patch of dandelions. they are a woman.
again, we are talking about girls.
always, we are talking about girls.
the specter of me having been one.
how she is downloadable now.
lives on a USB drive. wonder if
she's met anyone. when i take off the headset
he doesn't say goodbye just
"what if you stayed?" i think about it
until the moon is the only eye left open.
i think of putting my life
under my tongue. walking around
with blue jays for hands. sitting beside
my girlhood & putting a piece
of caramel in her mouth.

Robert Okaji

Something Else

If I shoved my arm through a slit in the sky,
what could I pull back into this morning?

Bits of ice and cotton?
Or that candied glow draping the horizon?

The one that smells like coals and burnt
earth and all the little insect husks

gathered at the sill. I close my eyes,
observe the pixels and veined patterns

my brain conjures to adorn night's
backdrop. Sometimes I dream in monochrome,

reels whirring in a projector's glare,
casting blurry shadows in the distance,

as though across the plaza through a Venetian
fog. Water accepts hues, reflects them

back to us, unlike smoke, which absorbs.
I once spent half a year squeezed tight

in depression's fist—every long hour choked
with a fine powder of crushed ash

and transparent fiberglass—until the day
my throat opened and color returned.

I reach for daylight, tall grass, the crescent
moon. Birdsong. Coral and granite.

The peace of an unfilled grave.
What I retrieve is something else.

It is all so real to me

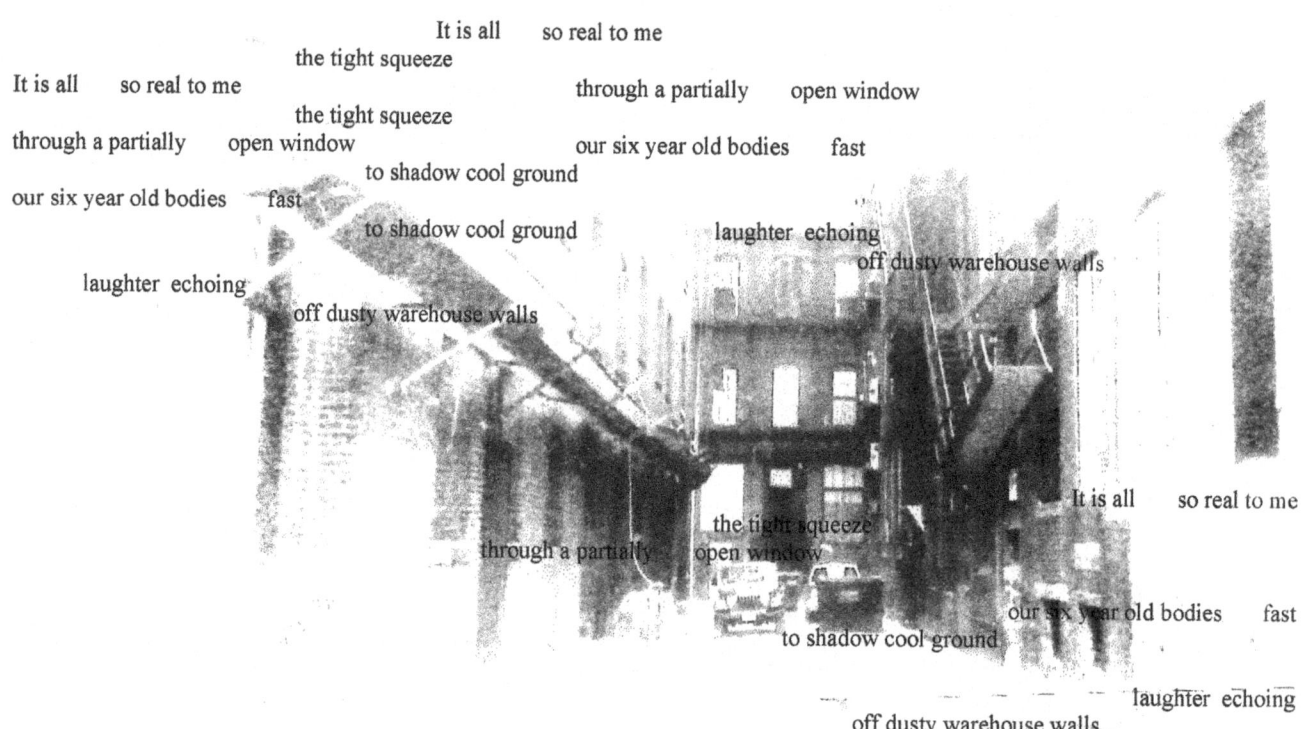

It is all   so real to me
the tight squeeze
It is all   so real to me
through a partially   open window
the tight squeeze
through a partially   open window
our six year old bodies   fast
to shadow cool ground
our six year old bodies   fast
to shadow cool ground
laughter echoing
off dusty warehouse walls
laughter echoing
off dusty warehouse walls

It is all   so real to me
the tight squeeze
through a partially   open window
our six year old bodies   fast
to shadow cool ground
laughter echoing
off dusty warehouse walls

OPENING SCENE

Facility of broken pods
→ One lone light w/in

Quinta as a shadow hovers over her.

GASP!

Quinta wakes up, blue light turns _pink_!

As Quinta gasps for air there is fighting outside

CRASH! SCREAM!
Her signature scar is created.

She struggles free, as fighting occurs in the background.

Quinta-VI: Introductory Scene—Storyboard 1 by **N'Dea Tucker**, 8.5 x 11 inches, digital art, 2021

33

The Extravagant Art of Seeing:
Thoughts While Tearing Up a Novel Late One Night (Page 12.1)

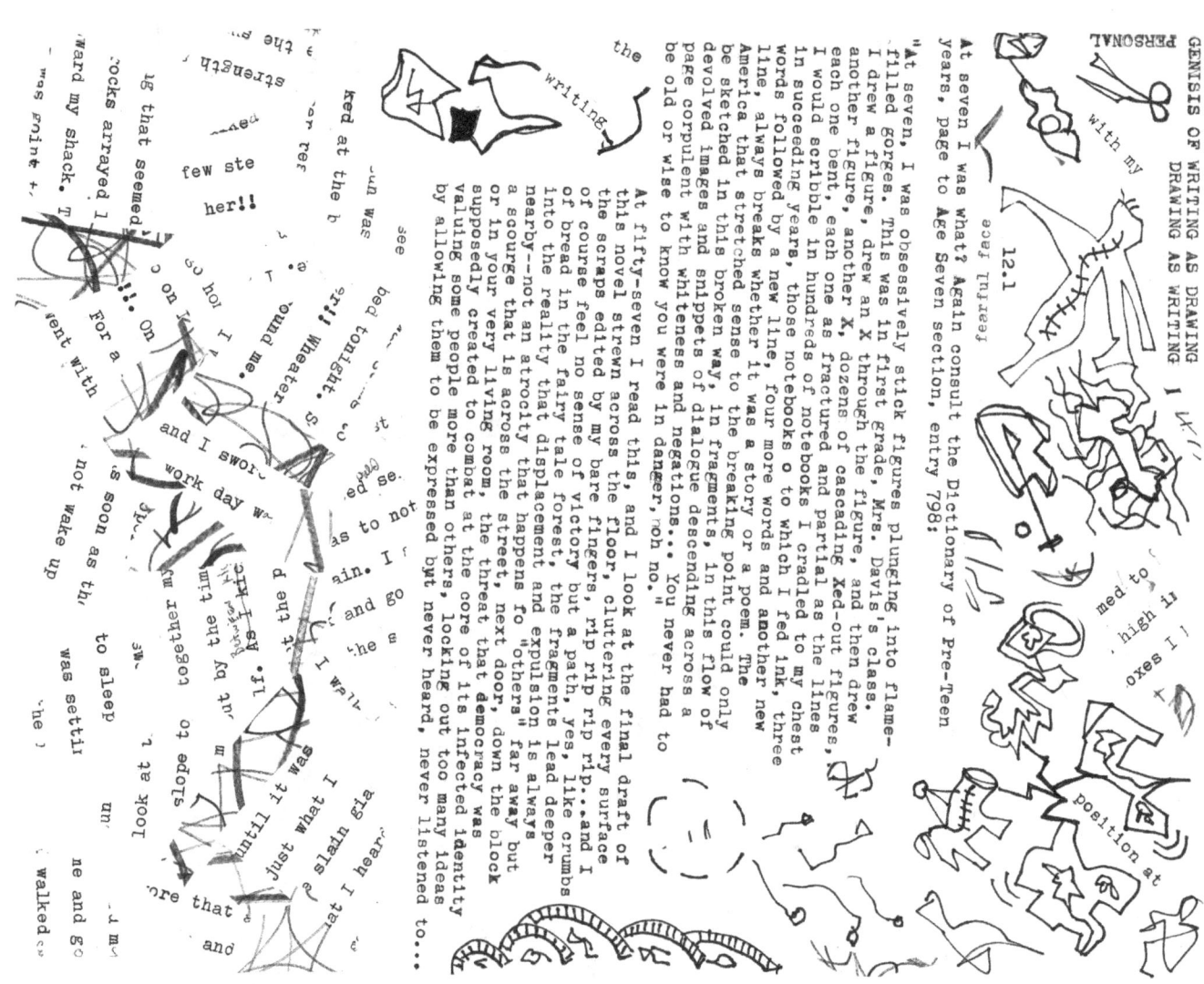

GENISIS OF WRITING AS DRAWING
DRAWING AS WRITING

PERSONAL

with my

12.1

At seven I was what? Again consult the Dictionary of Pre-Teen years, page to Age Seven section, entry 798:

"At seven, I was obsessively stick figures plunging into flame-filled gorges. This was in first grade, Mrs. Davis's class. I drew a figure, drew an X through the figure, and then drew another figure, another X, dozens of cascading Xed-out figures, each one bent, each one as fractured and partial as the lines I would scribble in hundreds of notebooks I cradled to my chest in succeeding years, those notebooks o to which I fed ink, three words followed by a new line, four more words and another new line, always breaks whether it was a story or a poem. The America that stretched sense to the breaking point could only be sketched in this broken way, in fragments, in this flow of devolved images and snippets of dialogue descending across a page corpulent with whiteness and negations... You never had to be old or wise to know you were in danger, noh no."

At fifty-seven I read this, and I look at the final draft of this novel strewn across the floor, cluttering every surface of course the scraps edited by my bare fingers, rip rip rip rip...and I feel no sense of victory but a path, yes, like crumbs of bread in the fairy tale forest, the fragments lead deeper into the reality that displacement and expulsion is always nearby--not an atrocity that happens fo "others" far away but a scourge that is across the street, next door, down the block or in your very living room, the threat that democracy was supposedly created to combat at the core of its infected identity valuing some people more than others, locking out too many ideas by allowing them to be expressed but never heard, never listened to....

Mispronunciation

She's tired of being afraid.
Afraid of trying words on
the wrong way and being laughed
out of town. Afraid of not
wearing them at all. Afraid *town*
is only a figure of speech.
Afraid *wilderness* is what
she really means and how
can she survive out of wilderness?
Afraid those bringers of shame
will come to haunt her years
from now, when she needs them
the least, and possibly
in a different language. Afraid
they will have disappeared
by then, leaving behind a mere
aftertaste of insufficiency.
Afraid that 'years from now'
is today. Afraid that today
all she has is a whole
wardrobe of words—predatory,
condescending, all-knowing.
Afraid she can't help
but love them as they are.
Afraid that love is enough.

Mahina and Me in Madness

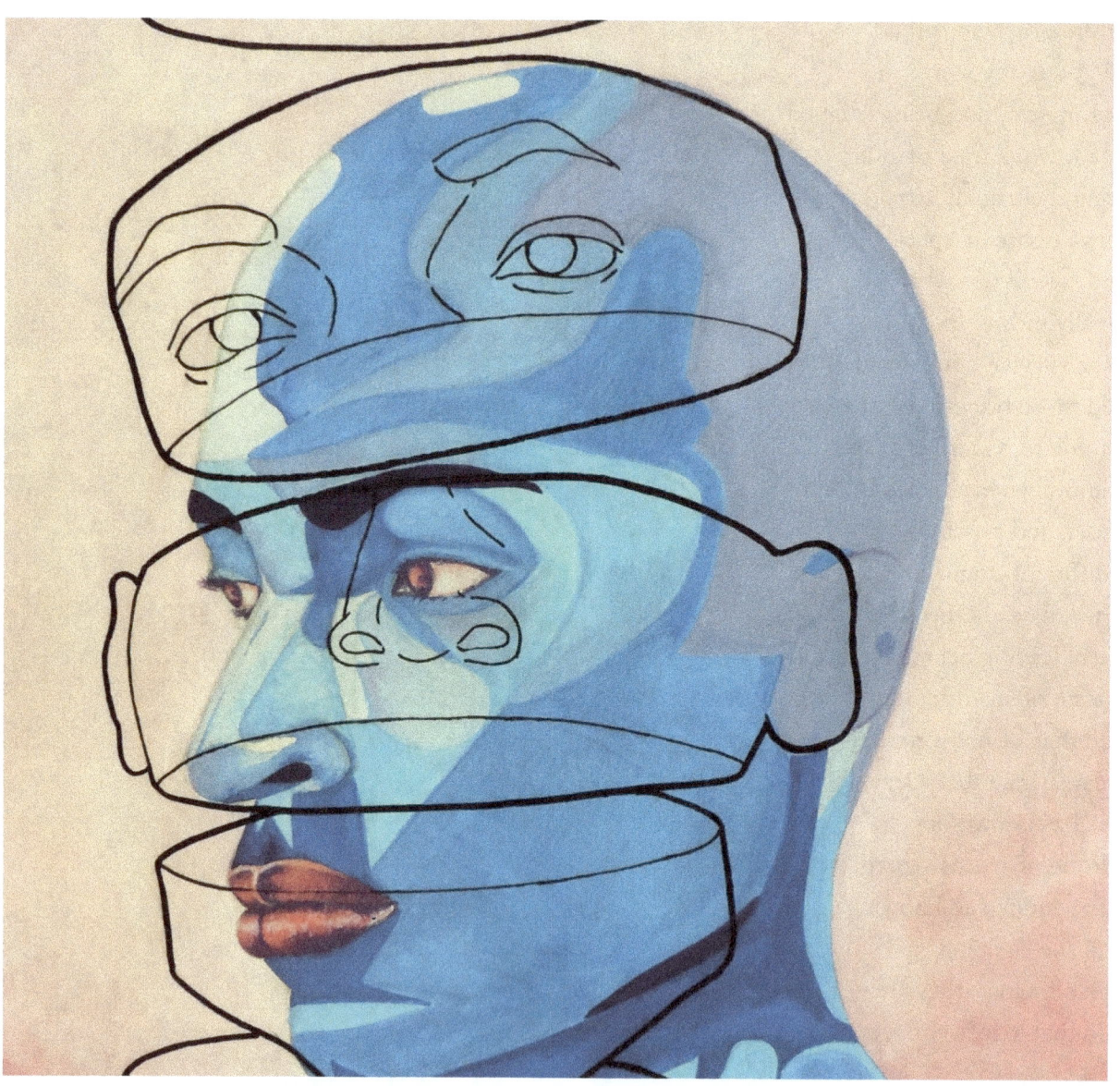

Boy by **N'Dea Tucker**, 8 x 13 inches, watercolor, colored pencils and marker on paper, 2016 (cropped)

We are inpatients in rehab, Mahina and I. Doesn't matter for what.

The nurses, surprised, say, you two get along. I speak her crazy, I say.

What's that?

You want me to … translate for you?

Sure, why not.

The first day Mahina talks a lot and I stay out of it. I'm too tired to even listen—rehab is a job. Until 2 a.m.

At 2 a.m., Mahina calls her sister. They chat, long and loud, as if it's two in the afternoon. Though I have insomnia anyway, I'm pissed.

The next morning while the curtain is open, I mention the conversation. Mahina denies ever making the call. But I soon replace her sister at 2 a.m. anyway. It's *always* quiet in here, but the dark is even quieter. We learn how to make our own noise.

The next middle-of-night, Mahina turns on the TV. I have mine off always, because my seasick eyes can't make sense of it. I turn over, gingerly, and stare at the dark, trying to remember what birds sound like.

The next middle-of-night, Mahina puts on her light and then falls back to sleep. These things might seem small, but listen and remember: I can't get up to move the curtain between us because of the bed alarms. I have to wait for a nurse. The next morning as I head to shower (I'm odd days and Mahina is evens), I pass her bed and say, you'd better not do that again. She laughs, and winks like a leprechaun, a sprite, a trouble-making fairy. The doctor declines my morning evaluation as she makes rounds. If I can throw shade at Mahina, she says, I'm doing just fine.

Mahina wanders in the night and sets off alarms—bed, chairs, doors. I scold her; the nurses scold her. The next night, she steals my wheelchair, which has no alarms because I'm a Good Girl. They catch her anyway. She winks at me, and dances over to therapy even though she should be sitting.

When Mahina acts up? What I do (and repeatedly practice just to annoy her) is reposition my bed. She hates that noise, and I smile to myself at what little control I am able to wield. If she sets off the alarm in the middle of the night, I spend a lot of time getting comfortable. Stay in bed, I tell her. Never, she says. I raise my mattress up and down once more, just to get the last word.

There is a man who screams for help each night. You can barely make out the word help in all his screams. He sounds like a bleating goat. Sometimes they have to call security. We're always awake for it. We're too far apart to hold hands.

We talk, make up stories to pass the time.

Our stories are outrageous—but in that room, they are no less sensible than the birds that must be out there. Nothing feels real, so anything could be real.

So for several nights, we are descendants of the elite, a wolf pack called the Arcadians who are fighting with the rival pack. The senior nurse is our Wolf Matron, though she never lets on. We'd be expelled from the pack if we mentioned it to her. But we exchange a knowing look when she takes our vitals.

Mahina swears she met a man named Myst when she first got here. He could perform voodoo. But then he vanished into literal mist. We mourn this because apparently he was very handsome. He never comes back. We expect his warm welcome when we re-enter the Pack.

Mahina has restrictions on both salt and sugar, and chocolate is out of the question. Her craving is real and lively. She reminisces about melting Almond Joy candy bars in a pan. The bars turn into chocolate coconut flat stacks, which you can then slide over ice cream or eat by themselves. She talks about this nonstop, and it becomes something of a joke. Before long she has myself and all the nurses craving Almond Joy in a big way. I order chocolate ice cream and imagine, trying not to gloat as my mouth bursts with sugar. There she is, making it sound like one bite would give us everything we're missing. It's magic, she says. I believe her. We dream, and we drool.

We eat everything together. She eats a lot of bacon in the morning; we can only get it in the morning, so she saves me two slices for lunch. We hate the steak and love the spaghetti. We hate the grilled chicken and love the fried chicken. One night I mistake my refried beans for chocolate ice cream. Mahina reminds me that even those beans would be transformed with a little Almond Joy on top. I finish the bowl.

One night she says, we could throw #2 pencils at the holes in the ceiling. Holes! This is why I dream of holes! I say. I'm always looking at the damn ceiling! When I close my eyes I see holes, always: coral, tree trunks, eyes of creatures. If I am dizzy at the time (which is most of the time), they move. Or is it me moving, shaking, rocking? I never can tell. Doesn't matter, because the holes are real, up there and down here. Through our eyes, and through our brains.

How about colored pencils, I say.

She says, #2 pencils aren't as dark as they used to be.

That's because there's no lead anymore, I say.

She says, I like #1 pencils.

I squint. The pencils would fall back down on us, I say.

She says, not if we threw them right.

This is what it's like: nothing but holes. We fill them, however we can.

Sometimes we giggle when we say goodnight, because we know we'll both be awake in a few hours anyway. If she cries I don't hear it. I don't cry. I don't have the energy to be sad. I'm working too hard to get out of here.

One day Mahina's ID bracelet comes off. Of all people, the nurses say, she'd be likely to do it on purpose. They should give us, Mahina says one night, furry handcuffs like in movies.

Like with leopard skin.

She says, yeah. I want pink ones with feathers.

You never stop, not even at 1 a.m.

Nope, she says. First it's voodoo zombies and next thing my bed's alive.

One day Mahina says she thinks we could solve some of these Cold Cases. I think back to my roommate at the last rehab: she watched so many of these—meaning *I* watched so many of these—that I'm sure I could. And Mahina is sharp as a tack. She sees kaleidoscopes, literally.

It's always the boyfriend anyway, I say. Then we start talking about wolves again, and the handsome Man in the Mist who disappeared. A great way to pass the time. A better way than thinking about what's been lost for years and will take years to recover.

Mahina checks out of rehab before I do. It's a Thursday, and the room is painfully quiet. Although I eat alone, there is freedom in the silence, and it seems fitting that I should end the way I started: alone and trepidatious, stubborn and determined. She entrusted me with these stories. She entrusted me with this courage. I won't let her down. There will be no Cold Cases here.

I'll fry up an Almond Joy for you, I say as she walks out. She says, You can try it, but I made it up. Doesn't it sound good though?

Carrie Vestal Gilman

Parts of Speech

Once   a little man   perched on my shoulder

which only   she   could see   because the door opened

only   for some   (he said looking down the long narrow hall)

who knew the code.   Then, his soul

left   from the side of his head   instead   of the front,   which

meant quite a lot   and

something ominous   to the newly grieving peony on the porch stairs.

Afterward and all day long   she looked for news   of her

father from the war.   Later,   when I asked how

he   was doing,   he said, "Oklahoma."   Lastly,

my mother (in the hospital)

questioned in a haze   of pain relief

if I'd found

the blue tape   and both of us   looked at the other

and laughed

our last shared laugh.   Words broken   in places where

beds have rails.

truths

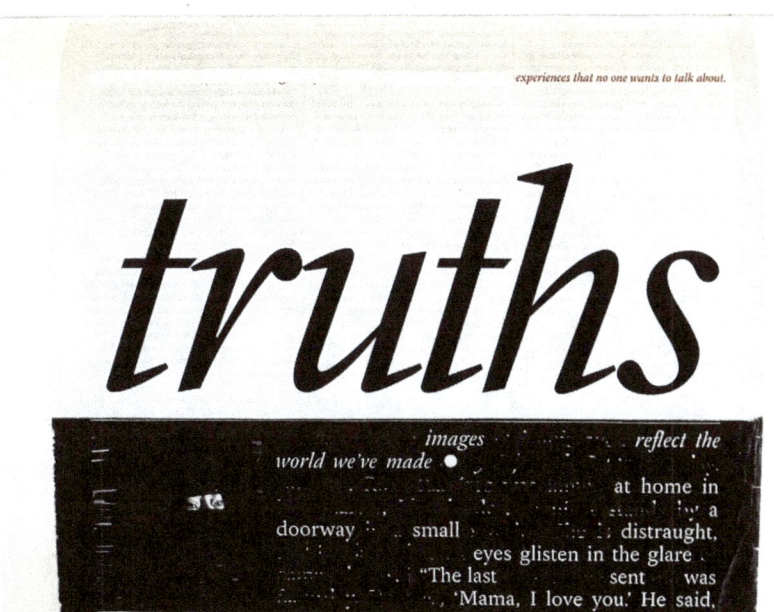

Dramatis Personae

Willi Tannenbaum—the speaker's given name, also known as Vladimir Ruchinsky, Vladislav Ruchinsky, Vladislav Ruchunsky—whatever will do.

Alexander—the archivist, the traveler, the translator, the director. He occasionally speaks.

Safta—Alexander's grandmother, whose translation and occupations he inherits.

Bronislav—the first to disappear.

Anni—Willi's Aryan lover, capable of vanishing. A relative. The heroine.

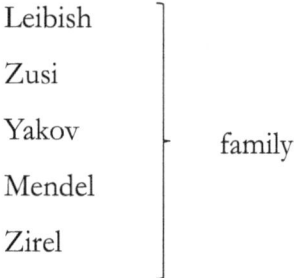

Leibish
Zusi
Yakov   family
Mendel
Zirel

Frania—the stubborn one

the soldiers—the chorus

the unnamed dead—the chorus

3. Her, why / how did she leave [when commanded] [when abandoned] [by Willi] / what is the meaning of brothers / of relative / the meaning of generous / of [my] precedence / it already so hard / what is a heroine / what of their bed / of my confusion [and the] success of history / what was before the war / had they found a translation for each other / synonyms for *Aryan* and *Jew* that rest together / in the bed of a sentence / did Berlin / what is the dream / did they burlesque together in lace / drag together in Weimar / did she predict the invasion of brothers / is she [Anni] my necessary wall / is moving a kind of wall / how did she [later] pass goods beyond the gate / how could he [Willi] write like this / how did I not remember / how dare he / what were the words behind her perfect hair?

1. Safta translated *Rutchinksy* as *Ruchunsky*. I first hack into *Haken*, as in *hooked nose* or *snagged*, as in a coat caught; then *kreuz*, the word's *midsection* or *cross* as in *Christ*. *Binde* as in *bandage*—I am ready for etymology before I learn, together, the word is simply *swastika*, and I learn the danger of compounds, of the *Arbeit* that goes into deconstruction. Safta adds the word *beautiful* before *blonde* within *eine blonde Frau am Arm*. The woman and the arm, like the city, are capitals, as language wants. The passive voice

```
Warschau. Eine Millionenstadt: da taucht man leicht unter, da
schreitet man sicher über das Pflaster. Entlassungsschein in der Ta-
sche: Volksdeutscher Vladislav Rutschinsky, für besondere Anlässe
eine Hakenkreuzbinde, eine blonde Frau am Arm, wat jeht denn mich det
Janze an?!... Rüttelt mich wer aus dem Schlaf: "Ihr Name?" "Vladislav
Rutschinsky!" würde ich ihn anschreien. Mir kann keener....
```

continues, as one does, one will. Safta's translation ends here but the language continues. Even the dictionary doesn't know: *jeht, det, Janze*. But *what* and *because* and *myself* come through, though I imagine him confident, walking the Warsaw pavement with swagger. The text says Willi is shaken from sleep, asked his name. He *would* yell at him "Vladislav Rutchinsky," an imagined show of strength. The dictionary doesn't know *keener*, but the online translator intuits the sentence means *I can't...*

2. *On the Town*, starring Frank Sinatra and Gene Kelly, follows three sailors that disembark into New York City for a single day. *It's a helluva town!* Like Warsaw, the city contains millions. The year is 1949. *Find the romance and danger waiting.* The sailors site-see, sing, dance, and chase women. *When you have just one day; gotta pick up a date...*they see the loves of their lives on trains, on posters, on stage *maybe seven or eight on your way in just one day!* To be in a city one must have a dame. *we've hair on our chests.* I've never seen grins so wide, the uniforms white. *a visitor's place, where no one lives on account of the pace.* The picture was filmed on-location, at Kelly's insistence. The Technicolor moves. *But seven million are screaming for space.* We enter the film wide, the pier worker narrating in baritone a softness. *The people ride in a hole in the groun'.*

One walks safe.

43

The Translator [~~Alexander~~ 9261994] Speaks

"there is no poetry after Auschwitz"—Theodore Adorno, *misremembered*

I grew up just to stumble. I called summer camp,
a place I loved,   *Jewish camp.*

Within me is a number [my birthday] divisible
by *chai* [18, life], which equals 514,555 lives
or if presented elsewhere from here, 1,449,555,
both with a remainder.

So, what overlaps? *I* and *ich* for one.
Itinerary another. We went to the place
with an unknown name [Oswiecem]:
the place where it happens.

I will be told that it is important
to tell his story, and so will be asked
what was the hardest part. Not to mention

the full synopsis, and who would I want
to play him in the movie, and could it be
Tony Shalhoub, because, you know,
he can play such a good Jew?

I'll admit I've been there [Auschwitz]. *Ich bin.*
Past a page [I won't number it] held
in broken binding [hunched spine], the room fogs,
envelops like a kind of smoke
stuck in the small.

I took the train
for convenience.

If I knew him [spoken, seen him, touched him] I'd know his bar code

and love, and estrangement's grammar. Anni
miscast by her brother as dead,
told in the afters to the survivor [Willi].

I am an evidence—*Ich bin ein Beweis*—
of time. A lesson I learn in a bombed city.

—I love too.
A woman I scratch elegies for
on the desk-wood and cutting paper.

In time Anni would find Willi married to a Jew [my great-great aunt].
I've decided this is a kind of murder.

I could never write a love poem.
I wonder too often how much, she and I, *[Sie, ich]*,
hold within us the dead.

how i arrived:
(after Eve L. Ewing)

1.

a dull redbird, muted
crimson bookend.
feathers lacking
shock of sun.
listenin' so hard
i fell out the tree
into womb.

2.

Ma was sick-a-me peckin' at her belly button so she ran a bath. heard wise say hot bath get baby out 'bout time it's warm. called her two tooker-toddlers to get Nana! when lil' lisps cried wha's wwong? she said nothing. she made noise. third tookitfromme-baby made her screech.

3.

i paid for that screech before us all left the coop.

4.

Ma found helping hands above her. found arm nestled at small of back. found Nana's embrace as she carried Ma   & me in my nest   & the ghost of Ma's tooker's mother in me   all us   downstairs. layed us all on couch.

5.

nearly by the grace of Nana's palms. suspicion of bashful ambulance prepared blunts, towels, bleach, cord-cuttin' shoestring, makeshift midwife ready at water's mercy. angels stationed.
        ambulance became brave.

6.

tired cardinal cap strained short of membrane. EMT declared my unveiling. said, "crowning! you're crowning! i see ahead!"

7.

hesitant.
tookitfromme's ghost-mother
had me by the ear.
told me secrets.
gave me her face.

Grasping for Hummingbirds

Who's Helping Who by **Shelbey Leco,** 11 x 14 inches, mixed media, 2020 (cropped)

He's the ghost, but I'm the haunted house. I'm the one betrayed by my floorboards, whose rafters creak and groan as winds howl through me. Yawning corridors labyrinthed within as he faded to nothing, slow as weeds on a grave.

When the haunting was confirmed, he rushed home—more corporeal than ever. He held me, we held each other, as blood ran down the walls, paint peeling and bubbling in its wake. We clung together, weathered through as pots and pans flew around the kitchen, as our bed carouseled through the air, as shadows devoured every light in our home.

It was weeks of this—months maybe—until one morning the pour-over carafe was where we'd left it the night before. The bed stayed anchored; the living room lights flickered then stayed on. We both shambled the rooms like Romero's finest, but with the new-found calm, I could sleep through the night again. He said it was too quiet. Said the absence of chaos was unnerving.

But he returned to work. That's what you do after credits roll, right? Go back to life? He looked better to outsiders—he smiled and laughed and went to meetings, taught classes. But his scent was off. Loamy. Rich and damp. I should have caught it then, but we were past the worst of it, right? Besides the occasional creak in my floorboards, reshuffling of my rooms, we were returning to normal.

Then one day, casually as mentioning a craving for fries, he said he felt a charm of hummingbirds had roosted in his ribcage. Constant buzzing, fluttering about. He flexed his fingers like snatching for a bird I couldn't see, then disappeared into his office.

I dreamed of footsteps through my empty hallways, but whenever I turned there was only dark. No moon. No stars. The smell of dank soil. I'd thought it a trick of the light, but as he stepped out of the shower the next morning, I swore I saw the curtain right through his chest.

Days later, even a shirt, a hoodie, couldn't obscure the hollow there. Movies always show you fading from the extremities—fingertips the first to go. But he wasted from his center, the very core of him. He grasped at hummingbirds, eyes glazing over through meals, while watching TV, while grading papers. When I asked, he just furrowed his brow, stared through me. Like peering through a fog rolling between him and my windows.

I dreamed of a child's laughter echoing through my vacant halls, bouncing off dry-rotting walls and floorboards. When I woke, a silent scream tearing from my throat, he was there, floating six inches from the floor, out the bedroom, down the hall. I followed, mine the only footsteps in the house. His head lolled to the side, his limbs dangling limp. I hoped he'd lead me to answers, an explanation for his fading away, but he drifted aimless through the rooms. A kid's helium balloon drifting out of reach. I pulled the dog from her kennel, climbed back in bed, and waited to wake up again. It had been a dream within a dream. But the sun rose, the birds sang out our window, and I was still waiting.

Weeks later, he was just limbs and a head—a barely visible torso tethering them all together. If I watched long enough, had the stomach to stare, I could trace the line of flesh as it crept away—receded to invisible. He kept working, kept smiling, but his eyes stayed glazed, and the stink of dirt and worms followed him around the house, clung to his clothes, fully tangible so long as he didn't wear them.

He talked and laughed, present enough when he turned it on. But he shifted into some standby mode otherwise. Just his head floating there, two hands and a foot all he had left to him. He still rubbed my feet, kissed me goodnight, but sometimes I felt his fingers slide right through me, his lips just a whisper. I knew those last visible pieces of him floated through the rooms as soon as I was unconscious, dreaming of cracked, spidering windows, decaying floors.

And then one morning he was gone. That smell still lingers in his pillowcase, the bedsheets, no matter how many times I wash them. In the evenings, our dog tucks herself into the corner, stares at his spot on the couch until bedtime. Now I drift the rooms at night, searching for a glimpse, a hint. A flash of his hair, his favorite pen floating above his desk, even a hint of that stupid twitching, grasping for hummingbirds. Some comfort of his lingering here. When I do sleep, I dream of long, dark halls, cavernous rooms. A silence so oppressive, so heavy I need my ears to pop. When I wake, the rooms are too full, air thick, gritty with the stench of peat. The walls choking with artwork, with knickknacks, with photographs. The specters of our years together.

He was the ghost, but my rooms are haunted by everything he left behind.

he at once let go

Relentless

Previous researchers have noted that asexual participants have, in the past, felt compelled to curtail their responses to queries about psychiatric symptoms in an attempt to downplay any potential relationship between asexuality and psychopathology.[1]

I can give out pieces of my heart and still be intact.
The sea whose shells we take, the sun whose rays
scan our skin through clouds. To reflect is to be
aware of oneself on an array of surfaces: shadow,
scent, snatches of expression on faces across
from yours. First impulse, then rationale as a person
reaches for you in passing with teeth bared,
barreling towards shifting canyon light. Points
of contact once secreted now spill. My eyes
rove from inside a stranger's sockets. Someone
slips you beneath a microscope without noticing.
I desire freedom from the structure that soothes.
My waxen limbs are always calm. Faucet drips
relentless upon a spoon-scraped bowl.

---

[1] "Mental Health and interpersonal functioning in self-identified asexual men and women"
https://www.tandfonline.com/doi/abs/10.1080/19419899.2013.774162?journalCode=rpse20

Joshua Kulseth

THE DEAD

But the dead are never all the way dead
the way you might expect a stone might
retain all its stoniness and in stillness
be only a rock, like a corpse might be
only a corpse, but the dead are never
just the dead. Instead, maybe like a key
death opens what might have otherwise
been a wall, a floor, but now a door
is keyed into by the departing person
not dead, nor fully alive, but something
other, like the spooned-out guts of fruits
dumped on the ground might fester
but the husks abide behind, hollowed
in the hallow of some sacred vessel.
and maybe the spirit still lives like the guts
chucked on the ground which fester
but the aroma at first pleasant lingers
in air like a helicopter silent overhead.

Elisávet Makridis

ENDANGERED DIALECT LESSON: FIVE REVISIONS

Η κοιλία μ' εγέντον λαμνίν.
My stomach has turned into a small knife.

Τρώγω την καρδία μ'.
I eat my heart.

Εγομώθεν η γούλα μ'.
My throat has filled up.

Εκεί 'ς σ' οσπίτ' αγουρέαν 'κι μυρίζ'.
In that house there is no smell of man.

Επεκρεμάγα 'ς σην γούλαν ατ'.
I hung myself from his throat.

Ας σο στούδι μ' έν' το 'κι αγαπίουμε.
It's in my bones to be unloved.

Ντο είπαμε να γίν'τανε άλας και νερόν.
May whatever we said become salt and water.

I.
My stomach has turned.
Into a small knife, I eat. My heart,

my throat has filled up. In that house there is
no smell of man I hung myself from.

His throat, it's in my bones. To be unloved,
may whatever we said become salt and water.

II.
I hung my stomach from his throat myself.
Filled up my bones to be unloved.

Into a small knife whatever we said is, has turned.
It's in there, in that house. May my heart smell

of no man. My throat has become
salt and water I eat.

 III.
That house we turned into my bones, to I.
"I become his unloved smell hung

from man," my throat said. Maybe
a heart of salt, no water, is in his throat.

Whatever my small knife has filled up,
eat. There, it's in my stomach and in myself.

IV.
Man, that house, has become salt. May his throat.
I turned into no smell hung from water unloved.

It's in my bones to be a small knife.
Said, "Eat my heart, my stomach."

Whatever we filled up has my throat,
is I. There, in and of myself.

V.

I turned his unloved throat into a small knife
and filled up my stomach. I hung myself

from my bones. Man, eat no heart.
Whatever my throat said, become, is. It's May. We salt

my smell. Of water that house has to be. In, in there has.

Transliterations of Pontic Greek expressions:

Η κοιλία μ' εγέντον λαμνίν—I kilía m' egénton lamnín

Τρώγω την καρδία μ'—Trógo tin kardía m'

Εκεί 'ς σ' οσπίτ' αγουρέαν 'κι μυρίζ'—Eki 's s' ospít' agouréan 'ki myríz'

Επεκρεμάγα 'ς σην γούλαν ατ'—Epekremága 's sin goúlan at'

Ας σο στούδι μ' έν' το 'κι αγαπίουμε.—As so stoúdi m' en' to 'ki agapioúme

Ντο είπαμε να γίν'τανε άλας και νερόν—Nto ípame na gín'tane álas ke nerón

Ecolalia

I want the last sound from the throat of passers by:

lala sing echo exasperation es this y eso es envisage en copia

sound repeated by reflections y can you believe he said said

sayings invocations in voices a symphonia erasing by steps de maíz

caliente maíz caliente maíz caliente summer rebounded in the facilities

of mind mine eso es miyo calmate ya concept a pictorial hallucination

intimidated by a pounding sun y tourists by the pier look down into

the water take a picture in the forms represented this likeness of

a moment this likeness of a moment copy pasted digitized even evening

lala sing echoes in maintaining form y maíz manipulating eso son miyo

can you believe she said y honk honk honk maíz caliente lenta lenta

y pararse ya wait for me i i honk honk maíz erasing the steps gazed down

and dawn this lala sin me mixed like noise all noise all noise all noise

the landscape of sound : the highway

you grew up in the always vague vicinity of highways, their mummified ambiguous textures coming or going at all times, you would leave your windows open at night to let their low hums drift in on the breeze. there was a lawnmower reliability to the sound, consistent and yet intermittently yielding, you didn't know you were falling in love, you were just trying to sleep. i grew into the sound grew through it, barnacles on the pile. probably because sometimes i think i hear sound within other sounds, i don't mean like dual tones, i mean like when the sound machine is on at night and playing which also sounds like the highway which also sounds like the ocean, i maybe hear a symphony playing somewhere far away or in one ear or sometimes as i am trying to fall asleep and listening to the machine or the cars sputter along the highway then rising out of motor churn is this violin, whining and body-like. and this isn't the losing of tones, that is where other sounds get quiet so that the tone that is about to commit suicide inside your brain can have just a few brief seconds of stage shining light, this isn't that, this is sounds within other sounds, or sound within amorphous sounds. like when i am at the beach and in the waves i can hear yo yo ma weening his cello and i sweep the sand looking for where he might be hiding, behind a low dune perhaps, but i am alone with the waves and the piece i was sure i heard him playing evaporated into salt heavy air. maybe what i mean is that i am aware of the sound within sound, this orchestral music, nicely audible when it randomly appears. but to be fair sometimes the sound within the sound is not music, sometimes you are sure it is your alarm, jarring at you from the other room while the house's central air fan whirs. sometimes i question, is this a lie, just a bored brain's trick, another worthless deviation but then it feels too real to ignore and i must search for the origin point to this unwelcome resonance. i search and search but finding sound isn't as easy as it seems, and i know that sounds crazy but listen, i know what is real and what isn't. don't go making that face. you are well aware that some sounds are real like the kettle leaning on the gas pedal and that others like the alarm clock going off throughout the day and like yo yo ma at the beach and like the highway halo harmonies and like the random orchestras interrupting the nightly noise machine are not. you know this because the moment you tune in closer to every noise except the one you are looking for, the sound disappears, the smoke tones turning to wisps in your hands. but then i worry that i have really lost it, that my brain is really starting to turn, that this is the hidden cognitive dissonance, a promise tied in uninfected blood, cropping up now, so yeah, there is a subtle fear in the degradation of my phantom sounds. but maybe you made all this up, maybe you are not hallucinating, and am instead just an ambient liar. but now it's audible. isn't it, those little pitches chattering their way in. now i hear it.

don't you.

don't i.

Still Life with Rorschach

steam-rolled

my head

but not without some

beforehand   consideration

regarding the ooze

not   merely the mess of it but   how

viscosity has a way of encouraging flow

shaping it into rivers or pools

when all you think

you really want

is to cut   yourself a little   loose but

isn't   that the   point

to be slammed

now and again face-first into asphalt

nothing left but

dark   against   dark

what we make of ourselves

no more   no less

than   what we can   make

of

contour and shine

ink   splat

on pavement

Cory Hutchinson-Reuss

Those Disheveled Peonies of Flame that the Fire shook over your Garden[1]

He has concertina wire fencing

He is inside
a sequencing, a sentencing

an imposed story of static & failure

In such a familiar way he disappears

/

The subconscious in May places him in a driveway from my adolescence, an open car door where he stands
I see him wish not to be seen

Time served, face tinted with a blue vein
pale & hot

A version of himself
as diminishing returns

Our dream mouths
offer no assurances

Even here it isn't so simple
Debted in a house of days repeating

[1] *Title from Break of Day by Colette.*

It isn't easy
to live by a different grammar

To forgive yourself is a scandal
                    to those who would keep you
                                        a fretting echo of your past names

I've been one of those
                                        A mind that loves a verdict

/

I thought I knew what monotony was
                    All the moves a narrative could make

        My done days
                    circumscribed by a house

                    & the self as the smallest
                    kernel of a nested doll

/

                    He writes himself as a limping wolf,
                    a swan, a mirror

He becomes a broken pane of sun on the yard
I fly impossible statements into low trees

The car has rusted, sunk into a garden

Windows missing

        Heat warps the air, source
                    unseen, scatters the plots

        into pink sound   into an iconography of bells, the pleasure of
tulip bevy, day thief, knife in succulent, the fire

                tosses its head to tremor
                  & bloom, to shift our fear

into color

into color   we're shaken loose

              /

He has crushed pennies from the tracks   Faceless coins for a wish to be thrown

I don't know where he'll end up   If his own voice will fling open like a hand

Isaac George Lauritsen

In the Nature Store

It winds aimlessly—a wilderness of perennial shoes
      in a green that exhausts my personhood

though I've consumed too much caffeine.
      Where's my heart? Right here, flopping towards you

as you appear from an aisle as if it's a cave
      and you have foraged a button to push a cuticle

and this small movement, which makes you undeniably you,
      makes my brain a caveman: *Me bonked with glad!*

I wish I could present to you a bird. Instead, I'll buy
      this store's inventory of moss and make a couch

for us to bask in TV's glow as if it's the sun we're under
      on a beach and we're the sand and before this we were rocks

and as rocks we came from the greatest mystery
      which at this very moment is the oldest it has ever been.

What am I talking about? It would rather me not say
      but it feels like inventing fire together as it begins to snow.

Snow

is the amalgamation of snowflakes,
meaning ice crystals once alone, soon amongst enough to fall
from the sky
  through the air
    past the trees
      to the earth into
        tiny waiting mouths,
athirst and agape.

Agapē, meaning love.
I can't help it, I mean, the thirsty love.

Climate is different than weather,
both brutal in the Midwest.
For one year we lived in a little town
with a record low of -51 Fahrenheit,
where skin froze in two minutes,
where we learned to never touch tongue to metal,
where me and my brother were the only Black kids there.

I want to be clear—
Snow appears white in color.

But truth: it's made of clear crystals,
ones at last loved enough, amongst enough to fall
from the cobalt sky
  through the bitter air
    past the hoarfrost trees

to the rimy earth into
　　my tiny waiting warming mouth.
I'd cradle the weight of my head into my clasped hands so I could gaze up, forever watch it all,
　　　　fall, into me.

Rime is one shape, amongst many, that a snowflake can take.
I learned a long poem by heart that winter.

Standing in line at the bus stop to return home from school one day,
mouth agape, head held back, snowfall my melted bride—
the white boy standing behind me calls me *nigger*.

OPENING SCENE CONT. V1

Fighting continues off-screen.

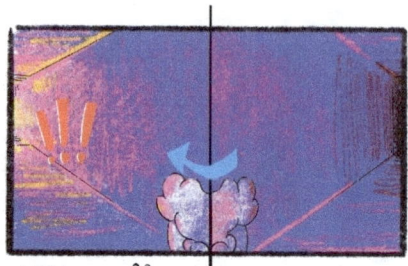

Which way??
Whomever is shooting spots her.!!

Camera follows around her

They shoot after her

Quinta-VI: Introductory Scene—Storyboard 2 by **N'Dea Tucker**, 8.5 x 11 inches, digital art, 2021

The Extravagant Art of Seeing:
Thoughts While Tearing Up a Novel Late One Night (Page 27)

Chkalova Street

The car belongs to my boss
Vladimir Pavlovich the Editor
in Chief. His driver (whose
name I was told but lost) is a
thick-necked hulk little older
than me with oil under his nails
and green-black tattoos on his
fingers. He says something
words flutter by but I cannot
catch them. This is not how the
émigrés spoke over extra-credit teas
voices swelling into small symphonies
of languid disillusion—*always
remember to use the formal, my dear, when
addressing your elders*—here everyone
speaks in rumbling bursts, gulping
words down before they end and
swallowing my comprehension along
with them. The driver turns down a
cobblestone street and stops and I
realize I must live here and get out.
I am starving. All I had to eat today
was bread salvaged from sandwiches.
Everyone here eats meat; that I cannot
since I've been ill makes no sense in
any language. I go back outside. The
stores are closed (not that I would
brave them) but there is a kiosk whose

light beckons from the encroaching
darkness. A few people mull about. I
feel them watching—clothes, walk
me: nothing fits. I start a smile. Stop.
That isn't done here. I point without
speaking. Two thousand seven hundred
post-communist monopoly notes
buy a bag of chips without the
chicken on them, what I hope are
some cookies and a bottle of wine.
None of this seems real. It is hard
not to run as I walk away. The
apartment's pink wallpaper and
red tassel curtains make me feel
like I'm Jonah inside his whale. An
old phone hangs on the wall
next to a radio with three channels
and no off button. I pick up the
receiver though there is no one
to call. Voices float up the line. A burst
of static sounds like laughter. I hang
up and then cut my hand trying
to open the wine bottle. Drops of
wine and blood mingle on the plastic
countertop, a Rorschach in red. I look
for a pattern that makes sense but
there's nothing to see except a
mess of my own making.

Arman Kazemi

Red dew

Jaleh, Tehran, September 7, 1978 – Sea-to-sky, Squamish, May 26, 2019

"My country turned as red with blood as a francolin's wing"
"At night he remembers freedom and flies in a dream"

Polka dots webbed the stones of a square,
plaited beads laced under an oxide dawn.
A city described in rusted turrets:
indifferent bodies that surmise the migrant
or the dead.

Russet caravans shuffled on adobe tiles…
A brick washer sprayed feather and carrion from quartz.
Sulphur spumes knit holes in flesh.
A kermes rug like marbled quarry
is spread.

The wine spangles annexed the turquoise air—
iridescent ligatures that scored the granite floor.
When the last guards vacate in cadmium pirouettes,
what's one perforated body in a history
woven red?

In the back of the Honda blown speakers wheeze Jaleh—
Oh dew turned scarlet coursing mad veins—
winding down the ochre sunset along the sea-to-sky,
the vast skein macadam unfurls
like carmine thread.

Beyond the opal sheet of Howe Sound
a plangent hawk winces its last dirge before the lead gift.
My mom in the side-view blossoms teal dewlets
as though hers were the broken wings that purpled
the square.

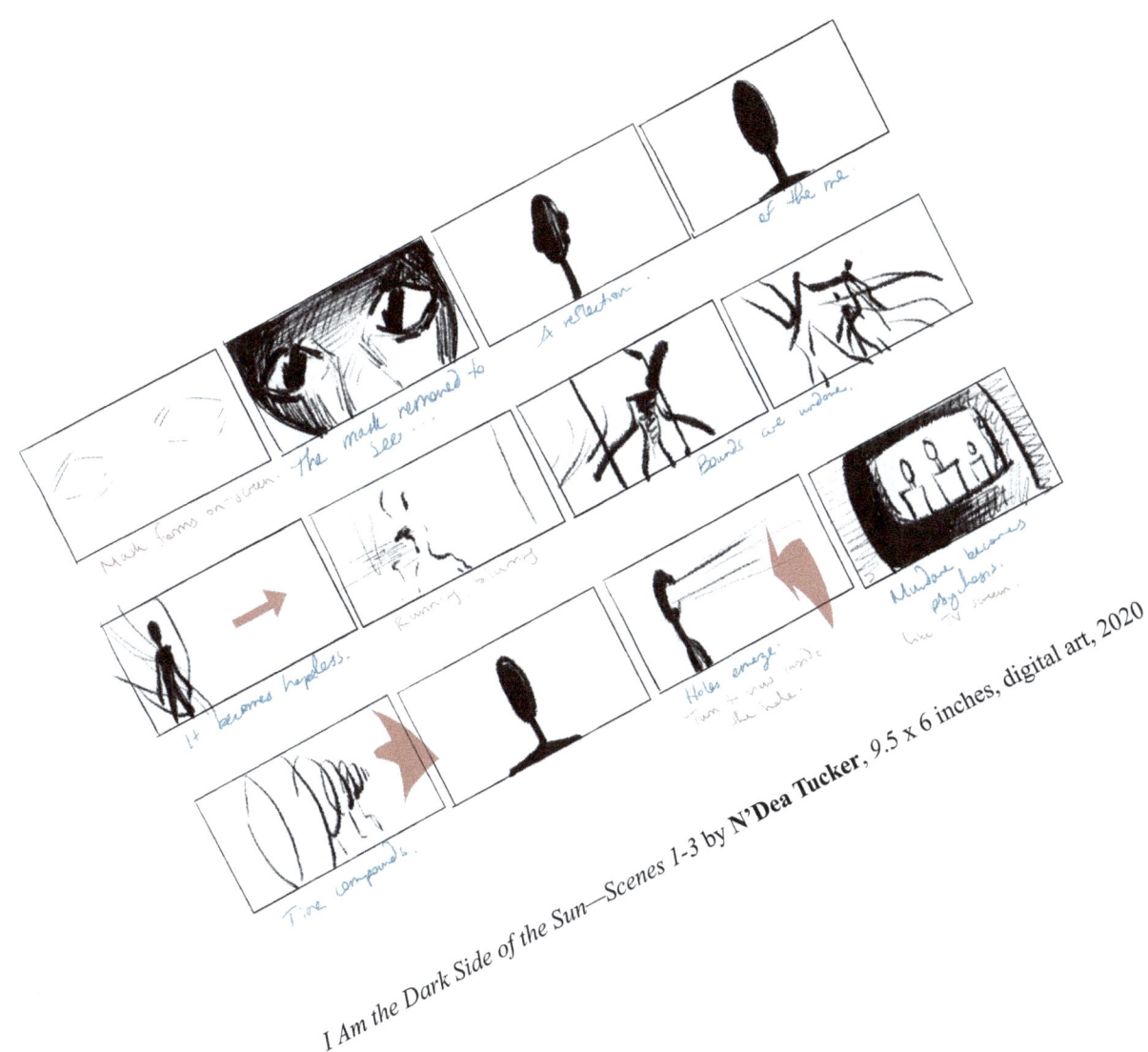

I Am the Dark Side of the Sun—Scenes 1-3 by **N'Dea Tucker**, 9.5 x 6 inches, digital art, 2020

Thru the Bottled Eyes of Sleepless

Where the centered valve of my forehead
faucets an uncertainty I wouldn't dare
apologize for, I picture your house. How
I can't help twisting the chrome-plated

tongue to its strictest borders of syntax.
Sometimes it takes both hands, until
I'm barely outlined in the late-day varnish
of dusk. I can't afford toy trucks rushing

in to crash our day. Nor can I provide
ample smallness to justify flowers. Observe
my once-and-future grave, how it flexes
our time-release lives, its paisley fillings.

With braking throttles open, where else
could I go? Doesn't everything awaken,
and too soon? I undo the radio of our verbs,
wear my toilet with a new delicacy before

my dented mouse fuselage disembodies
a song curiosity finds in me as I walk
past home, grow dim, nameless. To lose
everything a sort of winning, even if

at first it doesn't feel that way. Sinking
fills us like a ghost. I swim the tunnel
of your eyes until you jerk the valve, leave
me on the shoulder mumbling vowels,

TV smokestacks in pixilation. In the shop
window across the street, a tessellation
of heads spots me, pixies me into a matrix
your hallelujahs knock back in one gulp.

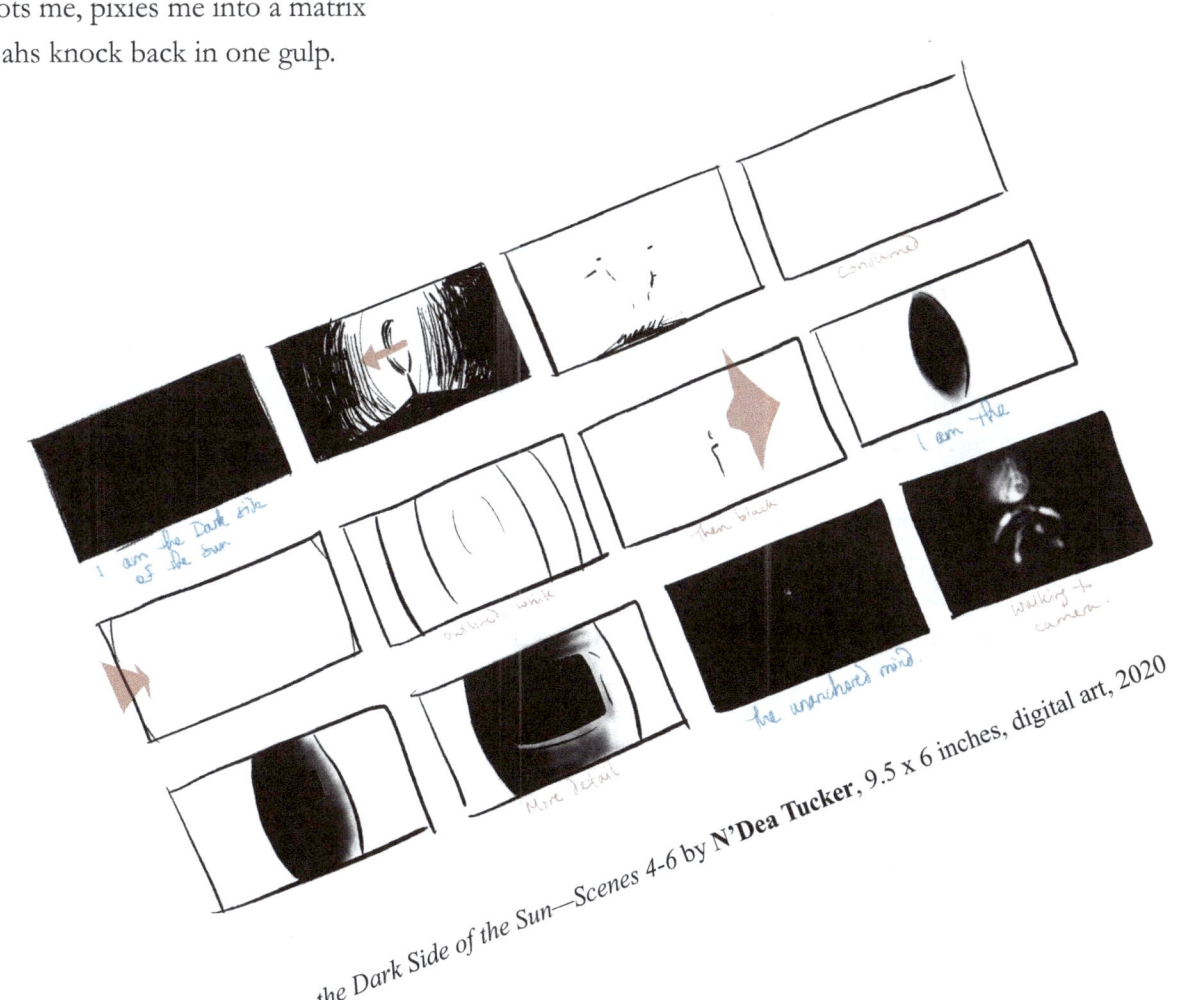

I Am the Dark Side of the Sun—Scenes 4-6 by **N'Dea Tucker**, 9.5 x 6 inches, digital art, 2020

WESTERN HAIKUS & AMERICAN SENTENCES FOR CORPORATE AMERICA

1.

morning sun
hidden behind menacing clouds
and i am awake again

laying on the bristles of the toothbrush, my tongue, not yet ready
   to speak

frozen
in the black snow—
a sweet cigarette

waiting for the bus ...
someone else here
longer than me

a man coughing. a woman yawning. the machine shuffles on
   concrete

Lake Michigan in the early morning is reflecting albedo

on New East Side—
303 E. Wacker Dr.
has no name

catching the elevator to the 40th floor, catching my breath

the office is fluorescent
white light walls of gypsum
& synthetic smiles

2.

desk after desk
arriving at my own
the red stain still

reflecting my distorted complexion, a stale cup of coffee

the chirping of Spanish birds, replaced by plastic keyboards &
  the phone rings

selling to people shit
they don't need, so i can keep
smoking weed

on the phone with Bob from Colorado … until he hangs up
  on me

lunch alone—surrounded by
rows of monoliths
& the species that built them

the length of a sweet cigarette
is not long enough
to keep me from going back

at the computer again, & my eyes burn against blue light

dull receptionist Lisa, will you listen to my misery?

when work is done,
i am the last
to leave, always

catching the elevator to the 1st floor, holding my breath

3.

a congregation at the city center: us superfluous whole

sent into evening &
spared of his labor—
a man lost on State St.

the poor
have nowhere to go
& i go home

on the bus again—the same sad faces i will see again
    tomorrow

rotting
in the black snow—
a yellow flower

Chinatown—
i live alone
in a basement

after shower fog
on the mirror,
i don't bother

nightfall, the apprehension for those menacing clouds,
    hiding the sun

Afterhours

After locking up, Millie always poured herself a finger of whiskey. She'd sit in the darkened bar, reviewing another night of awkward first dates, animated friendships, impromptu philosophizing, impassioned cultural critique, trivial dialogues, dedicated necking, live acts in the lounge trying their best to catch someone's ear, silent loners, scribblers, readers, obsessive phone scrollers, Saturday night couples coming in from the cold, revelers still restless after the after party and dancers, gleefully enlivening whatever space was their own, you know, the usual assortment whiling the night away. Quite a din on a good night, and Saturday had been a good night, so much so that the quiet was jarring, after the last patron had been turned out, the iPod silenced, the lights dimmed and the rooms drifting asleep. When the bar was awake it spoke en masse and Millie wondered if it dreamt that way as well, if all her customers' hopes and regrets lingered behind, seeping into the cracks of the floorboards. Millie never felt entirely alone in the bar, even at 4AM after last calls had been emptied and glasses left soaking for another night.

City of Coats

Tending the Sorrow by **Jane Williams,** 12.5 x 10.2 inches, acrylic on board, 2020 (cropped)

lothes walk north and south down State Street. Just clothes, no bodies. No faces. No arms. No legs, but like something holds them up. Winter coats resting on imaginary shoulders. Wool hats atop invisible faces. Boots stomping without feet. These absentees go, go, go in scarves, leggings, sweatpants, slacks, suits, jeans, mittens. Constant flow.

Exhaust. New tar smell. Steam rises through grates on concrete. Clouds follow passersby: perfume, cologne, cigarette smoke. Popcorn shop emits scent, and down another block, barbecue, Indian food, Chinese, pizza, and hamburgers.

Skipping. Amongst drum of walking, skipping. Not one pair of shoes, two. Two outfits mitten on mitten skipping by the drones. One outfit: white knit hat, ball on top, blue winter coat, striped wool scarf, and jeans. The other: knit cap, brown leather coat, scarf, and navy slacks. Their hats turn toward each other. As if, taking a look.

And then . . . as they come up to Broadway Theatre, leather coat outfit throws blue one into air, and blue coat, white hat, scarf, jeans twirl, swirl, spin before landing. Break into a seamless ballet. Nearby, honking, walking, and a train horn.

And trumpets play. The two swing, sway. Passing subway entrance and into the road, they jive, hop, step. Grey sedan slams on breaks, doesn't let up on horn, but blue outfit springs at car, up hood, up windshield. Runs back down, jumps toward brown leather jacket.

On skyscrapers and stone buildings, windows creak open. Headless torsos peer out. Others line behind department store glass. No footsteps. Every outfit stopping. Watching.

Blue coat's sleeves spread, floating. Brown leather jacket's sleeves spread, anticipating, ready. They embrace. Knit hats turn opposite directions. As if, a kiss.

Bodies of clothing fling from windows, run from department stores, restaurants, and charge from subway. Every outfit skips, shuffles. Cars quit honking and outfits flow, dance on pavement. Good and bad dancing. Flinging. Flailing. All accepted.

They move this way, that. Go with one partner then another. Outfits flying land on concrete and parked cars. Climb lampposts, swing around. Sprint up and down sides of buildings. Desire to dance spreads, incurable disease, down avenues, alleyways. Soon every outfit in city dances. Traffic and business halts. Hamburgers char. Popcorn burns. Teapots whistle.

And, blue coat and brown jacket embrace. Outfits dancing around them, stop, make a circle. Hug. Ripple effect. The city; jackets, shoes, hats. In one hug.

Yu Hsuan Wu

Stay together

I want to always recognize you
when you say the word "magnificent"
accidentally push down too many stones

I recognize the traces of your feelings
on the lower edge of the collapsed wall

I picked up a stone
felt that you were far away
I picked up the seven hundred and thirty-sixth stone
feeling that you no longer remember
being here

Finally I can concentrate
on building a tiny, pale stone house
without begging you to come in

Now, my hands are
empty
ready to set fire
at the end of winter.

The Extravagant Art of Seeing:
Thoughts While Tearing Up a Novel Late One Night (Page 14)

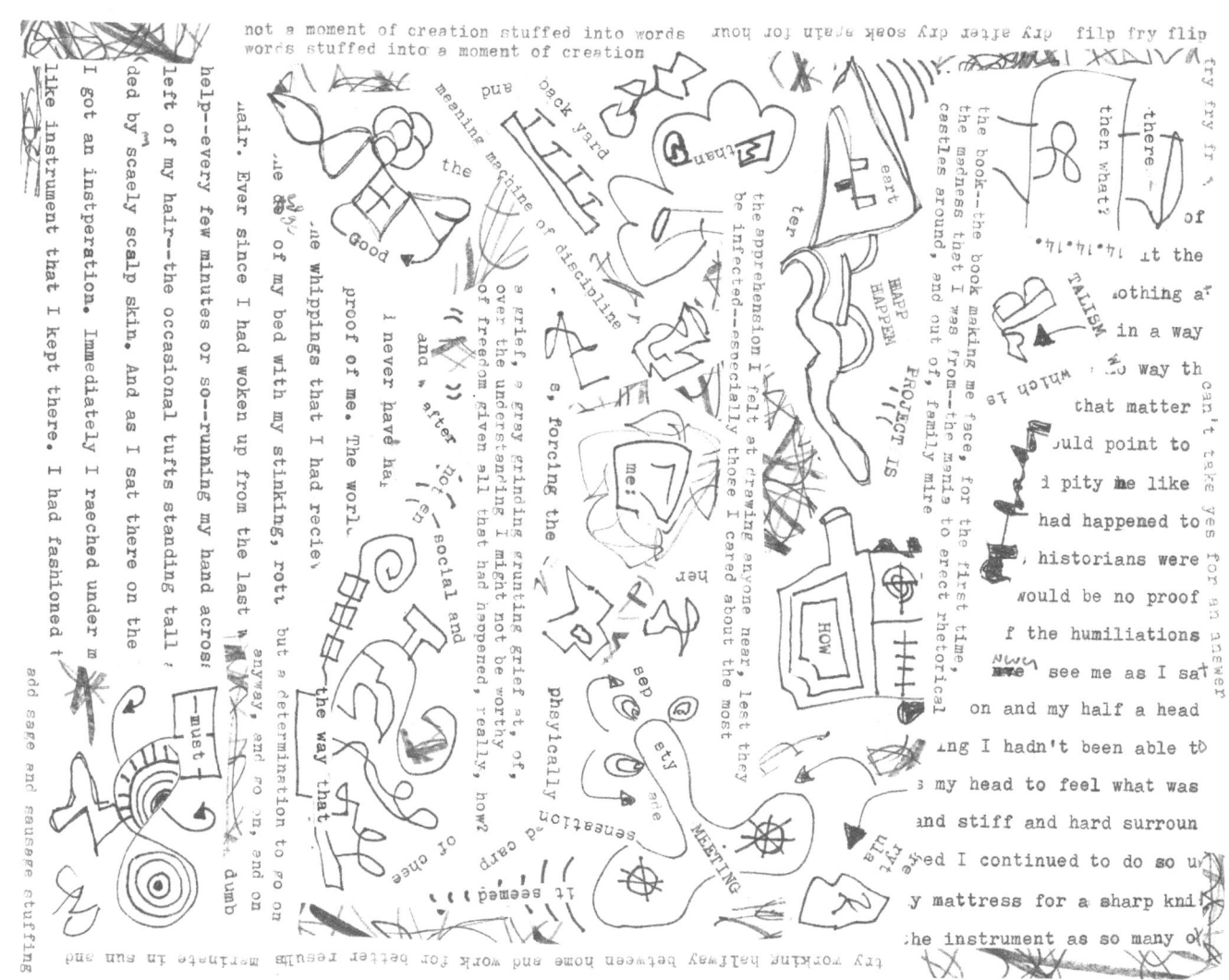

Jordan Anderson

waking

men tell me i
sleep too much, lying
 slanted along their beds like a
long black cat, a sphinx.
 i blink up at their heads--
little suns
 haloed by windows--
 and squint
 into the phosphene's
 negatives: here, gentler
  mouths that won't scoop at
 my drowsy helplessness
  with sour ringing,
  a tender punch
  to the cheek not held
 by my pillow.
  i can't seem to break
  this pattern, not since
  my first morning:
 my head out of
  the womb, my father
  saying "remember
  the way they showed you
  how to push? you're not
  doing it right."
  instead, i curve myself
  to their slight violence,
  like a woman
  in court. "i like
  sleeping," i say, and roll
  over on the mattress
  to match our faces;
  try to suck pity out
  from their eyelashes
  like honeysuckle.
  "i would sleep
   all day if i could."
   the cheek i've turned is
   oily from itself and
   the pillowcase,
   a shining lump
   of bronze for them
   to strike. my rebuke
   makes them angry in
    a way i don't understand.

when i was a child, i
would press my cheek
to the marble tiles
of the foyer floor,
a slide mounted
on wonder's microscope.
i'd watch the dust mites
like bubbles in cider,
smell the dry heat
from the vents. i could be
a little animal like
an unstretched
muscle. now, those boys
wake up before i do
and frown at my
slack jaw: they cannot
stand to watch the honesty
of something made
from them and nothing
else. they begrudge
a rib.
a long black cat
arches its back
to push its body
beyond the truth.
this is how i plan
to make them happy,
but i keep
offering up the same
stale sacrifice, no time
even to wipe down
the altar. the promise
busts my lip, and
the blood is like
sweat or the slick
of sweet, silent sex
done in the dark--
i can't handle any love
thicker than my eyelids
or louder than my sleep.
that could explain
the cruelty:
when i wake
up happy, they
have caught an infidel.

Mia X. Perez

The Siren of SoDo

Shark teeth and angel wings fall down
onto SoDo, the gas station

goddess arrested
with the chemical flow.

She: the siren of the goat song
tends the tendrils of her sugar

hair and commands the tides
—rainwater, butane, blood.

The city bleeds grey with her strange
weather, the clouds hunch low

and hungry. The bar birds
circle 4th avenue, dive between
coal trains, severed limbs

and methadone clinics
in search of the word

that might dispel her
umbilical dream.

five stages

grief is the realization of the loss of a dream -Ram Dass

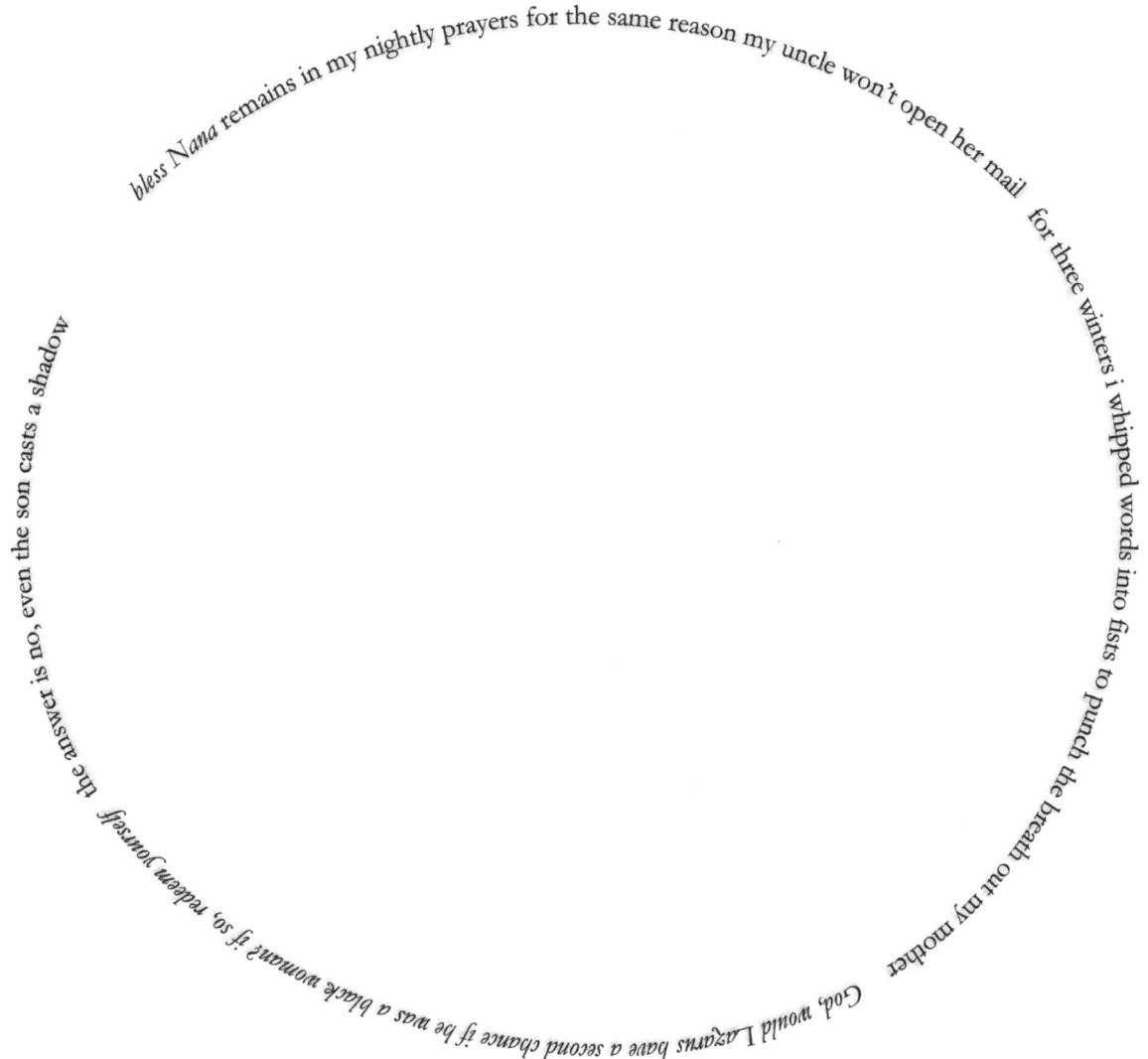

bless Nana remains in my nightly prayers for the same reason my uncle won't open her mail for three winters i whipped words into fists to punch the breath out my mother God, would Lazarus have a second chance if he was a black woman? if so, redeem yourself the answer is no, even the son casts a shadow

The Splendid Limitations of Being . . .

```
a        lone   a      l      one    all    one    all a   lone   a      l on e  all
all      alone  a      lone   all    lone   all    alone   all    one    a
one      all    lone   a      lone   all    a      lone    a      all    lone
alone    one    a      lone   a      lone   all    alone   a      one    all
a        all    alone  all    a      lone   all    a       l      one    a
ll       a      l      one    all    a      lone   on      e      all    one
All      one    al     one    al     lone   all a  lone    a      lone   all
lone     all    alone  a      lone   all    lone   all     alone  all    lone   a
one      all    lone   a      lone   all    a      lone    a      all
lone     alone  one    all    one    al     one    all     alone  a      one
all      a      all    alone  all    a      lone   all     a      l      one    a
ll       a      l      one    all    a      l      l       on e   all    one    All
one      al     one    al     l one  all a  lone   a       lone   all    lone   all
alone    a      lone   all    lone   all    alone  all
```

Allone allone allone allone allone allone allone allone allone

```
all      lone   alone  one    a      lone   a      on      all    alone  a      one
all      a      all    alone  all    a      lone   all     a      l      one    a
ll       a      l      one    all    a      on     l       one
all      one    all    one    al     one    al     lone    all a  lone   a      lone
all      lone   all    alone  a      lone   all    lone    all    alone  all    lone
a        one    all    lone   a      lone   all    a       lone          on     all
lone     alone  one    a      lone   a      lone   all     alone  a      one    all
a        all    alone  all    a      one    all    a
ll       one    a      ll     al     l      one    a       all    on     e
one      all    one    All    one    al     one    al      lone   all a  lone   a
lone     all    a      lone   all    alone  a      lone    all    lone   all    alone
all      alone  all    lone   a      one    all    lone    a
lone     a      all    lone   alone  one    a      lone    a      lone   all
```

The Splendid Limitations of Being Alone by **Shane Guffogg**, 48 x 60 inches, oil on canvas, 2008

the landscape of the river

there is something holding snow glazed over / the slip / you must search and / into fits and feathers / the the thing / you become times / the vicious promise to offering blistered clouds to / until it is able to drive claws that deceit / that lie you told shut down / the catacomb of violent it wants to be / you / lifting and lowering your pay the water no mind / not grandeur it desired / it was know that violence / it was spray / it waited / it was resistance to your placid the page / keep denying it an old lover to retain rights to they still do / and you know smile, a photograph no one deny the glacial run-off in its you down hard on the dirt, malcontent at this forceful feel it more / with its body so hold / you know it knows / down / dark and lurking deep / current steady moving freight train symphony highway above / this small helpless against tidal blood / and yet, logic shallow for a simple civilization that despite the manageable / yet you know this landscape / it could be as this frail carcass / tumbling the skull on a jutting stone / argue that then it was not the river knows the truth / it must be careful near the choose to tread.

there is something holding on here / the softness of old snow glazed over / the frozen-in tracks helping me slip / must search and dig for days / or i relapse / into fits and feathers / the artifact / the buried depths of the thing / i become distracted by the ice / like old times / the vicious promise to let me down / to bury me / offering blistered clouds to gaze at / draw closer / deeper / until it is able to drive claws into me / tying me down / that deceit / that lie / i am safe / shock and shut down / the catacomb of the river / i know how violent it wants to be / i want it so badly / to consume / lifting and lowering my head, a cow grazing / i pay the water no mind / not at first / not giving it the grandeur it desired / it was not my ocean / it did not know that violence / it was not the same wild winter sea spray / it waited / it was patient / could feel its resistance to my placid gaze / finger tips wetted on the page / i keep denying it though / the way one denies an old lover to retain rights to their body / but knowing they still do / i gloss over / and smile, a photograph no one takes home / i want to deny the glacial run-off in its stare / it wants to take / lie me down hard on the dirt, and drown / feel the malcontent at this forceful denial / in this valley i feel it more / with its body so close to mine / i know its hold / i know it knows / each hillside climbed up down / dark and lurking below / undertow / basin deep / current steady moving ice down / stream raising a freight train symphony against / the backdrop of highway above / this small body incapable of ignoring / helpless against tidal decisions born / into my blood / and yet, logic proclaims safety / far too shallow for a simple drowning / so close to civilization that despite the cold / hypothermia would be manageable / yet i know those tethers / stronger to this landscape / as simple as a foot slip / send this frail carcass / tumbling avalanche / only to smash the skull / and submerge / one could argue it was not the river that did me in / it was me / it was me / it was / wasn't it.

on here / the softness of old frozen-in tracks helping you dig for days / or you relapse artifact / the buried depths of distracted by the ice / like old let you down / to bury / gaze at / draw closer / deeper into you / tying you down / / you are safe / shock and the river / you know how want it so badly / to consume head, a cow grazing / you at first / not giving it the not your ocean / it did not not the same wild winter sea patient / could feel its gaze / finger tips wetted on though / the way one denies their body / but knowing they do / gloss over / and takes home / you want to stare / it wants to take / lie and drown / feel the denial / in this valley you close to yours / you know its each hillside climbed up below / undertow / basin ice down / stream raising a against / the backdrop of body incapable of ignoring / decisions born / into your proclaims safety / far too drowning / so close to cold hypothermia would be those tethers / stronger to simple as a foot slip / send avalanche / only to smash and submerge / one could river that did you in / but the arranged it all along / so you edges   you

FINALITY

I wish to say. I don't know how to say. I wish I knew how to say. I do know how to say but I don't want to. I wish I don't have to hurt you, but I must say. I know hearing me say this can't be easy for you. I wish I could make this easier with the words I choose to say, but I don't know how. I want to sit down and say nothing. I wish I could feel strong enough to say. I want to lie down and sleep so I never have to say. I wish I didn't have to say that I …

The Keening Air

Your naked body is soft,
And tumult is my fingers
On your flesh.

And I am kindled by light
Refracted through the leaves of trees,
Upon a shimmering silhouette of skin.

And I spit leaves,
When I remember,
My mantra: the keening air.

Prunus

persica

you think   I'm   the culmination

of your desire my firm roundness   matching the inner

curve of your hand the velvet sensation   fingers stroking downy

skin playing along the cleft where my flesh   folds when I'm ripe you

handle me with care my succulent pulp easily   bruised a gentle bite

and my juices flow mixed with your saliva yet   I am no metaphor

for human sexuality that is your imagination   my concern is

propagation eat my flesh expose me to the   core explore

the corrugated maze of my seed husk   scarify me

plant my kernel slide me inches   in to lie

in moist compost nurture   me and I

will grow and   bring forth

peaches

Jessie Pocock

SIX BEST FRIENDS

we touch our lips we touch our bodies we touch cigarette we
touch fire we touch gallons of rum we touch pine needles we
touch snow melt we touch rainbow bracelets, we touch second-
hand clothes we touch our belly buttons we touch the edges of
the driveway we touch the bears who meet us there we touch
your dad's pyramids we touch potato skillets at the pantry diner
we touch cinnamon ice cream we touch threaded colored glass
pipes we touch dirt weed we touch tape cassettes we touch pale
subaru upholstery we touch neon flashlights we touch magic
mushrooms we touch queerness we touch raves we touch vicks
vapor rub we touch monster truck rallies we touch meth pipes
we touch pain killers we touch white russians we touch wellwater
we touch lipstick we touch hitchhiking up we touch hot metal on
motor cycles we touch twisting our hair we touch braiding our
hair we touch burials in loaf n' jug lobbies we touch blunts we
touch menses we touch winter storm warnings we touch floods
we touch wildfires we touch skating out car doors we touch skid-
ding in frozen parking lots we touch rainbow falls we touch
frozen lakes we touch sand dunes we touch snowsuits we touch

The Extravagant Art of Seeing:
Thoughts While Tearing Up a Novel Late One Night (Page 21)

JORDAN ELIZABETH ANDERSON | *2022 Sublingua Prize for Poetry RUNNER-UP & FINALIST*
At the beginning of 2022, I produced a series of five rapidly-written poems on the themes of my life in light of my father's recent death, "waking" being the second. While the poem is about my destructive tendency toward fawning, it's not all desolate self-pitying: there's irony in, for example, imagining sleep itself as a cuckolding rakehell. Though I hadn't yet read it, Terry Eagleton's book *Radical Sacrifice* aptly conflates psychological concepts of neurosis with the religious idea of ritual sacrifice, mirroring the way ***"waking"*** analogizes my own fear of risk and eagerness to please to a bloody altar on which "all ritual sacrifice ends in failure." ***"native girl"*** was written later in the year, stylistically somewhat inspired by my old teacher, Timothy Donnelly. It attempts to hop the stones of the paradigm by which I ultimately must learn of my "own" culture through the same source as its colonizers, at the Metropolitan Museum. Because poems like this one extrapolate a bit dramatically from my real life experiences, writing them is bound to feel silly at some points, but I'm assuaged in remembering that Thom Yorke claims to write his most genius lyrics the same way. Exaggeration is our job.

LISA BERLEY I begin with words, then visuals and vice versa, to create poem/collages by deconstructing and reconstructing found images and words forming new structures. The grief is fragmented and nonlinear, and writing with found words shapes the poem/collage's with the use of redaction, juxtapositions, punctuation, and abstracted visuals that more clearly express my tragic journey. These poems/collages are taken from my manuscript, *finding Nefesh* about my journey through grief, a 'collage of loss,' after the accidental death of my younger son in 2018. The erasure poem/collage ***"truths"*** (16 x 11.5 inches, sourced from the NYTimes' magazines) is about witnessing the changes experienced in grief, integrating the acceptance of living without him and the isolation I feel since his death. The word collage ***"he at once let go"*** (22 x 30 inches, collaged from fragments of the NYTimes magazine and black ink on paper collaged onto Arches paper) is a recent change in my approach to the poetry work, beginning with collage and then integrating the declarative words. This approach brings me full circle back to my roots in the visual arts.

DOMINIC BLANCO My work has become increasingly experimental. I now use the whole page, still images, arrows, & stretch language as if it was a clay. Rather than imposing a narrative where the 'I' has something to say, I resists the urge. This best summarized by Daniel Borzutzky, who wrote, "I prefer to think of language as being "informed" by experiences rather than being "about experiences." I write now with the trust that I have the knowledge & vocabulary to speak to how they inform my present. ***"WESTERN HAIKUS & AMERICAN SENTENCES FOR CORPORATE AMERICA"*** was written in 2020 during the first fourth of lockdown. I just moved out of a basement in Chicago, Chinatown. It took a period of time to understand what that experience was, that one can't while it is—The piece itself takes place in the latter half of 2019. I needed to separate myself to understand how absurd it was to go into office 5 times a week pre-pandemic. At large the piece is about capitalism, the stagnation of the middle-class, the mundanity of following a pattern. Separated into 3 three sections, it reflects the arc of morning into night, the realization that you will have to do it all over again.

CREIGHTON BLINN I always carve out a specific time during the week, usually a weekend afternoon to focus on something creative. Within that time, I work on whatever needs my attention and/or is sparking my inspiration. I may have an idea to start a new composition or revise an old one. I might practice my performance skills. What is essential for me is allowing flexibility. Composed for a series of character sketches set within a Brooklyn dive bar, *"Afterhours"* is part of a series, *Social Drinking*, that consists of four pieces, mixing prose and poetry, unfolding over the course of four nights (Sunday-Wednesday). "Afterhours" serves as a prologue centered on Millie, the bar's owner. Conceived and written during the spring/summer of 2020, the series is set in the days leading up to the initial Covid shutdowns. The pandemonic is never explicitly referenced in these works, as they reflect the period when most of us were still shrugging off the virus as irrelevant. Instead, my goal was to convey what so many of us took for granted in our everyday lives before Covid sparked its disruption.

OISÍN BREEN My practice takes three major modes. The first, my long-form work, is all about thinking and dreaming, until a broad concept forms, much like novel-writing. There is planning—though no plan survives the process intact—and, at times, storyboarding, followed by research, writing and editing, editing, editing—it is sculpting music. For mid-length works, the process is similar, albeit with less plotting and mulling, and more visualisation, for I see them as 'still-life' pieces, in a sense. Lastly, my shorter works either come from a medium-length work that has, forgive the bombast, revealed itself (as this poem, *"The Keening Air"* did) as best when pared back, or they come through collage, when I work with saved and pruned phrases and ideas to find music in new combinations. *"The Keening Air"* is a sketch, hewed and rehewed that developed alongside a longer-form book-length poem—my current major 'work-in-progress.' It speaks for itself, but I would add there is a wonderful sensuality to explore and inhabit in it combining the natural world with our own visions of desire. Far too often we forget this, in this age of atomisation.

ROHAN BUETTEL My writing process usually commences with an idea for a poem, or a feeling that I need to write about something in particular. If the subject is in nature or a physical object, usually I begin with free verse lines based on description and associations. Occasionally a fully formed poem will come out requiring little revision, but this is rare. Usually, I also research the subject, taking notes, often themselves in the form of poetic lines. I think about the best form to support the content of the poem. If nothing inspires, I revert to random techniques, like a random word generator, setting rules for myself about the use of the generated words. This approach can lead to some delightfully surreal outcomes. I wrote *"Prunus perscia"* after one day, mind wandering, I remembered a television advertisement in the 1980's for an Australian brand of jeans called Amco Peaches. The ad would juxtapose images of a peach with women's bodies wearing the jeans. The idea came to me to respond from the peach's perspective. Writing the first draft in unpunctuated free verse, I started thinking about form and experimenting with turning it into a concrete poem, which ultimately proved successful.

MICHELLE CRISTIANI Everything I've written about my stroke recovery came first from notes I'd taken at the time. Some of these are barely legible because I couldn't hold a pen very well; but once I could, I began journaling again, and I wrote constantly to practice my handwriting and re-teach my right hand how to work. I'm left now with notebook journal entries to piece my story together. But I copiously wrote down everything I experienced. So I'm lucky, because despite my faulty memory and scattered attention I can piece together most of my experiences. ***"Mahina and Me in Madness"*** is based on my inpatient rehab experience after a stroke at age 42. After this stroke, I relearned how to walk, talk, eat, swallow, and more; I was in rehab for 30 days. Three months later, I underwent two craniotomies for an aneurysm. A memoir piece about my first week post-stroke, "Blessed Are the Breathing," was published by *Calyx press*. To follow these vignettes, I am working on a full-length memoir that parallels my journey of recovery with the perseverance and determination written into animated hero tales. I'm thrilled I can tell these stories that otherwise would have been lost in gray matter.

TODD EVANS Writing ***"City of Coats"*** was improvisational and spur of the moment. I sat down at my typewriter without any sort of prewriting and tapped into what it feels like when I feel joy. I tried to recreate that feeling in my body, mind, and emotional state. I asked questions such as: What sensations am I noticing in the body? How would I describe those sensations? I felt a giddiness, an excitement. I asked, what adjectives describe my emotional state when I feel joy? And peaceful, fun, playful came out of that. That's how *"City of Coats,"* a story about items of clothing moving in synchronicity, came to be. My process for other writing projects is similar. I tap into a feeling, pair that with a subject matter I'm interested in, and start writing. *"City of Coats"* is a fanciful flash fiction piece. It's fun, joyful, and a quick read.

XANDER GERSHBERG These poems are part of a series that represent my multiple ways of reckoning and making sense of two documents: my great-great uncle's (Willi Tannenbaum) German-language memoir and my grandmother's (Safta) imprecise but essential English-language translation. Each form represents a different methodology for sifting through the layers of mistranslation and generational trauma that do and don't reside in my own body. In all, I consider myself a translator, while more literal in poems such as ***"City Life,"*** where I narrate my translational intervention(s) and include them as layers of commentary. This method mimics the Talmudic-practice of Mishnah, wherein commentaries would surround the original text, with each layer addressing the multiple layers that came before. ***"Dramatis Personae"*** is my attempt to register the names within the memoir's foregrounded drama. ***"The Translator [Alexander 9261994] Speaks"*** is my first attempt at finding my own body. At first the recording of the archive's details felt straightforward and technical. As I permitted myself to intervene into the content more bravely, both in voice and form, I felt an unspooling of threads within me that I struggled to catch and observe. I have, thankfully, but the process remains ongoing and slow, as it should.

CARRIE VESTAL GILMAN | *2022 Sublingua Prize for Poetry FINALIST*
My writing is frequently influenced by my experience as a social worker. Poetry offers me the ability to further explore the language of loss which I discuss daily with those facing medical challenges, who are a constant inspiration. Recently, I've become interested in attending to spacing on the page as a way to deepen meaning. ***"Parts of Speech"*** began to take form in a Lighthouse Writers Workshop with the poet Victoria Chang, on "Syntax in Poems." The challenge here was to use several subordinating conjunctions that allowed the story to move forward but with a nonsensical plot. I became interested in creating a collage of bits of conversations I've had over the years in my work as a medical social worker and in my personal life in which the actual words being said don't convey exactly what's happening, but the feeling behind the words does. My wish was to break these pieces of dialogue into their smallest parts to find new meaning and connection. As I wrote, I realized that the commonality between all of these moments, in addition to the

way in which language couldn't capture all that was happening, was that somewhere in the background was a hospital bed, a bed with rails.

ROBIN GOW I often think of poems via the idea of "entry points." In 2022 and even before that I often found these "entry points" into poetic exploration as places in which I find language unfurling or coming undone. Daily, I keep track of pieces or fragments of speech or words that I keep turning over and wanting to dig deeper into. These poems are a result of that excavation. These pieces are from an ongoing series of poems I write right after I wake up in the morning. I think they channel a lot of the liminality of the time of day. These also tend to be the poems where I explore subjects like family, queerness, and belonging through surrealism. I let the veils between reality and fantasy ebb and flow. For *"scavenger hunt,"* I was weaving and splicing memories as well as peeling apart the strands of connotations and meanings those words can have. Similarly, with *"VR brother,"* I wanted to push those two words together to examine my relationship both with my siblings and brotherhood and with virtual reality technology.

JENNY GRASSL This year I finished *Magicholia*, a book adventure in bipolar illness. Momentum builds and sustains me during a project like this that is ongoing for more than a year. The process was fluid and steady, although I felt anxious about revealing this part of my life. The book is out there in submissions, and has yet to find a home. Right now I am between projects, trying not to fear the void. It is exciting to have many possible directions to take, exploring freely. I wrote *"DIARY OF DEER WOMAN"* as part of a series for my book manuscript, *Deer Woman in the Dining Room*. As a woman with antlers, I found ways to express situations in my life with more clarity. The imagination focuses the most precise lens.

SHANE GUFFOGG Throughout my career, one question has formed the basis of my work: What do thoughts look like before we attach language to them. This simple question has led me to create numerous answers in the abstract rhythms of line, form and color. My work begins with an impulse toward the gestural movement. When the movement is translated to canvas, reason starts its dance. The first series of brushstrokes become the starting point of which the patterns are based on. In the body of work from the 2000s, which I refer to as my pattern paintings, the patterned shapes are created by the mirroring of the original gesture, appearing as a symbol system approaching a kind of writing. These shapes become patterns and are mirrored and repeated, often 144 times across the surface of the canvas. I always start at the top left of the canvas and paint from left to right, as if I were writing a linear narrative in English. These patterns are a microcosm of the macrocosm that I like to think of as a universe of thought: the "collective unconscious."

ISA GUZMAN My creative process this last year has been a continuation of grappling with memories and language. This year has seen a focus on the topics of culture and health. I've been learning to delve more into research, especially archival research, as a means to inspire and develop my knowledge around these topics, especially in its direct relation to me. In writing *"Echolalia,"* I continue a long-term project of trying to capture and investigate the concept of memory, and memory as related to my childhood in Brooklyn—an attempt at the former essence of the gentrified neighborhood of Los Sures (Brooklyn), a long time Puerto Rican enclave. Memory, especially of place, is a collapse of images. When I walk through my area, I can see what is there, while seeing what was there. I try to hold onto the images that repeat themselves—the echos that keep going.

JORDAN HONEYBLUE I use form often as a gateway into my poetic pieces. Form provides me with more creative innovation due to intentionality. It challenges me to expand my vision and voice. Some of my pieces are sparked by one line that comes to me in dreams or a thought that hits me randomly. This one line won't always end up as the first line, but it is the heartbeat and does find a purpose somewhere within the poem. With visual forms like *"five stages"* I found myself feeling like a kid again. Writing words upside down and placing lines strategically as cycle categories brought a smile to my face. I wrote *"five stages"* to introduce myself to my own grief after losing my Nana. At the time, I knew the process I was experiencing to be "grief," but I had difficulty *realizing* my grief. After drafting experimentation, I observed that my grief cycle is an incomplete circle with an exploratory blank left for "acceptance." Possibly, if and whenever I do make it to acceptance, that's when I could truly live the epigraph's sentiment and *realize the loss of that dream*, and have the courage to dream a new one.

CORY HUTCHINSON-REUSS Before the pandemic, I would go to my favorite coffeeshop to write. Now most of my work takes place on my couch. My process has included repurposing material from older poems, assembling notes from my journal and working them into hybrid pieces, trying out archival and epistolary forms alongside lyrical pieces and prose poems. Instead of starting with a bit of language and building a discrete poem, I've moved into a process of amalgamation and flow, gathering fragments, some kind of paraphernalia poetics. *"Those Disheveled Peonies of Flame that the Fire Shook over your Garden"* and *"Green in Prism"* are poems that emerged from the time I spent as a volunteer in the Writers Workshop at Oakdale Prison. The group has been on indefinite hold since the pandemic began, which has intensified the isolated conditions of incarcerated individuals. The poems try to attest to their presence, embedded in others' thoughts and dreams, and their presence as embodied writers and artists living in a system that often renders them invisible.

ROMANA IORGA There's a direct correlation between reading someone's words and writing my own. It's as if another poet's language coaxes mine out of its shell. I like to lose myself in language, so that the boundaries between who I am and my words become permeable. I can only write when I'm lonely, but when I write, I feel the least alone. *"Mispronunciation"* is a confession, a love letter to language. I'm a non-native English speaker and certain sounds in English are more difficult for me to pronounce. When I'm tired or in a hurry, my accent thickens; the sounds coming out of my mouth fail to reach their ideal shape. I mix up short and long vowels, emphasize the wrong syllables. It doesn't seem like a big deal, but for someone acutely aware of living on the periphery of her adoptive culture, this is a sore subject. It's hard not to think of my own tongue as unreliable. And yet, I'm drawn to words and their castles in the air. I long to live inside them, if only for a moment. When I write, I'm at home. It is a temporary home, but it is mine.

NITA JADE Creating anything during the 2021-2022 year was motivated by necessity, curiosity, the yearning for a creative release, and the need for all the dead birds to mean something. *"how i arrived"* is largely inspired by Eve L. Ewing's African diasporic poem of the same title in her collection, *Electric Arches*. I thought of my infamous birth story and zoomed in on the roles that my grandmothers played in my arrival:

one damn near birthing me, the other ushering on another plane. The red of the font is symbolic of these sacred ancestors, the blood that left them, and the crimson wings they grew.

ARMAN KAZEMI A poem starts not as an idea but a combination of distinct words or phrases that tend to suggest an idea. The words in *"Red dew"* were suggested by "Zhaleh Khoon Shod," or "Dew turned to blood," about a street massacre at the start of the 1978-79 Iranian Revolution. The song came on during a weekend drive, and my parents-children of that generation-broke into heated debate about the minutiae of that day, September 8, 1978; but my mind went to the words and their burning emphasis on the red dew transubstantiated to blood. My mother's tear as she recalled that day and the stained tiles of Zhaleh spring from the same source. Zhaleh (literally, "Dew") is the name of a square in pre-revolutionary Tehran where peaceful demonstrators were shot by forces of the Iranian monarchy, an event which many consider the beginning of the revolution. In the song, the dew of the slain becomes seeds of blood that blossom to overthrow the king. In the poem, the splayed droplets form a red tapestry that folds together the bodies of the dead with the survivors driving across the Sea-to-Sky highway. My mother's teardrops echoed the blood that scores squares in Iran to this day.

MAURYA KERR Despair these last few years over our nation's dual pandemics of Covid-19 and white supremacy compelled me into new poetic territory. I am so fortunate to be part of a writing class that has been, and remains, instrumental to the development of my craft—without their support and direct, concise feedback, I wouldn't have the tools needed to put articulate voice to that despair, or be published poet. *"Snow"* (and *"My black"* forthcoming in Fissured Tongue Series) are part of a larger group of poems about my experiences in the world as a mixed-race, light-skinned black woman, set to be published as a chapbook entitled *MUTTOLOGY* in March 2023 by *Harbor Editions*. Among many intentions, the work strives to look at the multitudinous ways of blackness and being in the world. I am invested in normalizing blackness by setting our entirety as beautifully quotidian, instead of the current racialized extremes of nadir or zenith, invisibility or spectacularization. I've long reckoned with my light-skinned blackness—the privilege and safety it affords me, but also its unbelonging and confusion of in-between-ness—and these poems live as part of that reckoning.

JOSHUA KULSETH Whereas my "process" used to be more sporadic and eclectic (meaning I took inspiration from everyone and everything, and wrote when I was able), having completed two book manuscripts, my writing is now more pointed, insisting on complete projects with definite themes. I no longer write with individual poems in mind, but rather, with the aim towards books.

KS LACK | *2022 Sublingua Prize for Poetry FINALIST*
My writing process revolves around the logistics of my illness—transforming potentially destructive constraints into constructive ones. I've jettisoned larger formats as my capacity has diminished, but feel the stories I'm left with stand stronger from the winnowing. I take more breaks, allowing my works to gestate differently. If the words I reach for sometimes lay hidden beneath a fog, the idiosyncratic nature of my fractured language leads me to unexpected formulations. Perspective and perseverance are key.
In *"Chkalova Street,"* I wanted to capture the nightmare panic of taking a test when you can't even read the words. I moved to Kyiv in 1994 to help start The Mirror Weekly (aka ZN,UA), Ukraine's first independent

newspaper. I was woefully unprepared for their reality, but my new colleagues adopted me anyway. "Chkalova Street" is from "Kyivsky Waltz | Київський Вальс," a poem cycle based on my time there. My friends are still in Ukraine—publishing, fighting, not giving up. To know more about ZN,UA and/or support their current online publication, please go the GoFundMe fundraiser, "Support ZN,UA".

CHIME LAMA (འཆི་མེད་ཆོས་སྒྲོན།) The way my ideas collect is like a Japanese shishi-odoshi (deer-scaring) water fountain, filling up and spilling over. When there get to be so many ideas, I have to do something. At times I am struck with an idea that I have to pursue sooner or later. The more compelling an idea, the sooner it is created. That being said, sometimes ideas, though compelling, need a certain amount of time to incubate and germinate. Meanwhile, less weighty poems could be conceived of and created more swiftly. I like to experiment with tools. While this poem was made on InDesign, I also like to use a typewriter, mixed media, my scanner and manual manipulation. I hope to make more tactile poetry of varying sizes that can shine and move/rotate in the future. *"Complete Phase Cancellation"* depicts two sine waves of the same frequency that are 100% out of phase, resulting in the complete cancellation of one another. The matter in question is how to love and move on from love as much as it is about how to move on from love and continue loving.

ISAAC GEORGE LAURITSEN Right now I'm writing weather poems. I recently moved back to the Midwest after living in the South for a long time, and the seasons are on my mind. "Defamiliarizing the familiar" lurks always around my writing, and a simple theme, I find, works well for highlighting the strange in the everyday. *"In the Nature Store"* is a couple years old, so I'm not exactly sure where the initial idea came from. However, as with most of my work, I'm interested in mashing ideas together, sometimes complimentary, sometimes opposing, and though I won't claim I knew I was doing this at the time of writing this poem, it was pointed out to me by a friend that this poem goes from a "consumer/environmental" poem to a love poem. I like when poetry does that—when it redirects, surprises, creates uncertainty so that by the end of the piece I don't have one feeling but a number of them. Strangeness, delight, humor, a playful, loose approach to language—just a few of the attributes that emerge when a poem works for me, both as a reader and writer.

SHELBEY LECO My artwork, *"Who's Helping Who?"* is an examination of who we are behind closed doors, when we let down shields/masks we put on for society and we are most vulnerable within that personal environment. It is a self-exploration piece of mental health self-stigma in the realms of: I believed (in moments) my illness was fault, that my friend would never be able to "get me", that it ruined my life, and it made me feel so ashamed. This is a self portrait. I've depicted myself on the left, and my friend on the right. We are in his bedroom. My brain is exposed, bleeding, and damaged. This represents the physical daily challenges I face as a person with epilepsy. The purple pyramid represents the mental/psychological challenges I face: depression, anxiety, and behavioral issues. My friend opened his home up to me during covid, and my epilepsy was getting worse due to high stress. He was helping to take care of me, which represents the duality in color. The eyes, his increased sense of perception even though he is sleeping.

RAYMOND LUCZAK When I start writing a new book, especially with poetry, I like to set up new parameters and/or limitations. For instance, in order to convey the sense of incompleteness I had felt with my hearing family (I'm deaf) for my book *once upon a twin*, I avoided trying to use the word "and" as well as rarely using uppercase letters and punctuation. In *A Babble of Objects* (*Fomite Press*), I often incorporated the visual elements of the object being discussed into the poem itself. And so on. Honoring such limitations requires a lot of problem-solving, which in turn forces me to think differently when I create new poems that I couldn't have written otherwise. My hope is that each of my poetry collections would feel different from each other, as a musician might strive to accomplish with each new record. *"FINALITY"* was part of my ongoing experimentation in the prose poetry form some years ago, and in this one, I was interested in playing with the challenge of trying to find the right words needed to break up with someone and yet explore the feelings of not wanting to go through with the breakup.

ELISÁVET MAKRIDIS | *2022 Sublingua Prize for Poetry WINNER*
The writing process for ***"Endangered Dialect Lesson: Five Revisions"*** involved researching colloquial Pontic Greek expressions that spoke to my family history, translating them into English with the help of my relatives, and intuitively scrambling and re-assembling the translations on the page. The poem was inspired by the need to reimagine linguistic fluency as the making of an interactive space between myself and an ancestral language I do not speak or write in but whose frequency made me. Pontic Greek (also known as Romeyka), a Greek dialect in danger of becoming extinct, was spoken by my great-grandparents and grandparents alike but not transmitted past their generations to mine yet spoken utterances of the dialect exist in my psyche. What kind of touch-work is possible between my English and ancestral tongues? What can be reconciled or regenerated in such entanglements? For this piece I took seven common Pontic Greek expressions, recycling language inside the limits of the English translations over a sequence of five revisions in an attempt to conjure a more pliant mode of language-learning, of tuning into the language behind language. The speaker of this poem is both mine and not: matrilineal in essence, it's spoken by Yiayiá X (Grandmother X) after my great-grandmother Χριστίνα, for all the women who've preceded me. The result is a Rubik's Cube-like play that re-visions the debris of intergenerational trauma and possibilities for healing across English, Pontic Greek, and (hopefully) a third affective language. It is a gesture of calibrating ancestral communion, a towards and with always-arriving.

E.A. MIDNIGHT I have these ghosts of myself always speaking. I love the communion, but as a neurodivergent person, it can be hard to be in service to the safety of oneself and be a writer. Writing asks you to go deeper into your catacombs and sometimes that is also where all the dangerous parts of yourself live. ***"the landscape of the river"*** (accompanying image taken with a 35mm film Minolta camera on Spine Rd in Gunbarrel, CO, 2018) echoes how it feels to live with two sides of yourself talking at once. This piece showcases an interior and exterior voice trying to break free from the pulls of depression and suicide that [still] have their claws in the narrator. The river runs through the poem, a cold reminder to be careful with your edges. ***"the landscape of sound: the highway"*** is a meditative conversation between the two sides of the brain, "i" / "you," about hearing sounds and the questioning of one's sanity. In a way, these two voices are talking to one another, but they also are speaking with the reader, engaging them. As these selves recognize the limitations of what they know [or don't], the photograph bordering the text tells us that what haunts us can occasionally also hold some light.

BEN MILLER I employ varying approaches to developing visual texts without the use of software, but one element unites all: the aim of offering the audience a transformational experience, just as each expression makes me, in some sense, a new kind of artist. By "new" I do not mean shiny and flawless. I mean possessing the piquant freshness of having been altered intellectually, emotionally, and spiritually by resolute immersion in a creative process. I created the first layer of my manuscript, *The Extravagant Art of Seeing,* by tearing up pages of a novel draft to create hundreds of scraps. These were glued (at many angles, but generally in sequence) on pages of 8 ½ by 11 90 lb. index paper. Next I generated small petroglyphic images (black pen on white paper) responding to questions: *How many new forms might space created by a work's destruction make possible? Does the maturation of expressive ability depend as much on looking backward as forward… piecing together a complete record of creation incorporating the poorest, as well as the brightest, content? That is, has the worst work the power to teach a writer the best lessons?* Images were then cut out and, along with typed text, deployed like bandages (or stitches) in and around the novel's shorn tissue.

ROBERT OKAJI | *2022 Sublingua Prize for Poetry FINALIST*

I'm a half-Japanese, Texan poet who finds himself, after a major life-upheaval, living in Indiana. Having left my home of thirty-seven years, I find that although circumstances have changed drastically—locale, climate, economics, culture, opportunities, relationships—the writing still emerges from the same curious place it's always come from. I seldom know what I'm going to write about when I sit at the desk. A word or phrase or simple image will pop out, perhaps influenced by mood or life's odd occurrences mixed with etymology, landscape and observation, and the spark ignites. I ride the flame and smoke where it takes me, and at some point, perhaps after only a few words, but sometimes after many lines, the poem starts taking shape. That's when it becomes interesting, and the real work (and joy) begins. With *"Something Else,"* I thought it might be interesting to express color by using sensory input rather than explicit words for colors. Hence the imagery and references to smell and texture. And of course over time and through revision the poem transitioned from mere descriptions to a memory of the intense feeling of a sudden release from the dark cloud of depression's grip.

COCO OWEN I like to work with language's promiscuous polysemy, in what Bob Grumman called the "infra-verbal" space. This practice gives me a "slant" way of reading and of seeing. It is also something of a compulsion: I'm fond of unravelling and remixing letters and words to surface their homophones and faux amis. My subject matter, if there is such a thing separate from style (serious question), is an examination of gender in all its multifarious means and ends. I love playing in this space of doubled vision—once opened, it can't be unseen. I was drawn to LA-based artist Shane Guffogg's painting, *"The Splendid Limitations of Being Alone"* when I first saw it. The title drew me in too, enacting a marriage of "splendid" and "limitations." The painting's title declares straight out that everything is constrained and that this is "splendid": the net creating the tennis game; the meter making the poem. Digging into the title inspired my infra-verbal ekphrastic poem. When I went even deeper into the title, into the one word "alone," I glimpsed the dance of the All and the One—the lone inhering in other. Those strange attractors.

ARIA PAHARI My writing process relies deeply upon observation and absorption of external sources such as reading, traveling, and hiking, as well as interactions with strangers, friends, and animals. I try to cultivate a practice of both immersing myself in and withdrawing from the world, since I need both experiences to write. I try my best to proactively note down ideas for poems or specific lines and images as they occur to me so I can work on a draft later. On the other hand, I also recognize when I need an encounter or impression to marinate for some time before I attempt to write about it. Other than making sure to consistently write, revise, and jot down notes, I resist having too many hard-and-fast rules for myself since I find that too many of those suck the joy out of writing for me. *"Relentless"* speaks to straddling multiple facets of one's identity, and harboring a protectiveness for oneself and one's marginalized communities. Asexuality has been historically invalidated in healthcare settings, and combined with stigma around mental illness, this erasure looms all the larger for people who are both asexual and non-neurotypical. While writing this poem, I allowed myself to amplify, rather than "curtail," my response to a hypothetical question about psychiatric symptoms as an ace person.

BOBBY PARROTT My poems are gently and sometimes brashly surreal, their leaps an opening into a space where the reader and poem may interact and be changed, a place where consciousness and art may recognize one another as impermanent loves and glimpses of the Real may be encountered. Sometimes words can become artifacts more than signifiers toward particular meanings, and texture may interact with sound and emotion on levels where individual identities no longer reach or oppress the freedoms we already possess but have forgotten along the way. In *"Thru the Bottled Eyes of Sleepless,"* I explore the way writing and mind interact, the mind a sort of "valve" to limit perception to the point of rationality thru the restrictions of language, and how as writers or readers, or thru artistic expression, lets say, we are often able to throw off these temporary limitations of convention and duality and enter into a space where our bodies are no longer what we are, a realm where infinite awareness is recognized as, lets say, the screen onto which our experience is projected, albeit momentarily during this human manifestation, where the "Real" normally gets progressively further and further away from infinite awareness.

RALPH PENNEL All through 2021 and 2022 I have been focusing on defamiliarization, gazing at texts through an ecocritical lens as a way of reframing and retelling, in an attempt to acknowledge that the "material world is a dynamic and innovative place that creates us even as we interact with and recreate it" (LeCain). Though in many ways the pieces here are a precursor to my current work, they are also its exigence. *"It is all so real to me"* is a hybrid piece that combines visual and literary texts. The image I shot for a completely unrelated reason many years before. However, when the true form of the manuscript the poems appear in revealed itself, I began to review ways some of the works could speak in tandem with image and I wanted the text to speak through, not about, the image. In Foucauldian terms, I wanted to "divorce both the figure and the text from themselves and isolate them from their space." *"Frame"* is, in Deleuzian terms, an assemblage of "frames" within a creating and delimiting out-of-field "frame." Both pieces are part of a larger manuscript in which the "stanzas" are framed.

MIA X. PEREZ The writing process begins when I become inspired by an image, often a particular setting or landscape that feels emotionally resonant. My first drafts can be several pages long or may never exceed a few lines. The important thing is that I have enough material on the page to start exploring. One of my favorite fun facts is that the word "text" comes from the latin *textus* which means woven thing and over the past year that etymology has been a meditation for me. Rather than forcing stories to emerge from a single idea, I've learned to seek out the frayed edges of my drafts and pull at loose threads so that I might weave a cohesive picture out of various points of view. The goal is to let go of logic and lean into emotional, perhaps even sensual, movement. *"The Siren of SoDo"* is set in the industrial district of Seattle, WA and follows the siren—here, an urban, ambiguous, half-conscious being—as the surrounding environment is consumed by her melancholic spell. Inspired by the history of SoDo, this poem speaks to its preindustrial past as Seattle's tidelands as well as the struggles of the marginalized communities who continue to live there.

JESSIE POCOCK My work explores the intersections of memory, sense, and exposure. *"Six Best friends"* recounts images and experiences that visually read like a running slideshow. The box form is meant to contain the experiences in a ridged structure to capture the multiplicity of traumatic, joyful, and confusing memories in the context of reconciling childhood lived experiences within the confines of adult life.

JESSICA REED In 2022, I'm revisiting Borges, Paul Celan, and Emily Dickinson, and I'm excited about Daniel Biegelson's *Of Being Neighbors* and Madhur Anand's *Parasitic Oscillations*. I've also been remembering a motorcycle tour of Rome with Tom Andrews, a remarkable poet who died far too young and is the reason I became a writer. *"Compton Scattering"* is a term for when the energy of a photon is transferred to an electron after a collision; we know this because the photon's wavelength changes. The physical chemist and philosopher Gaston Bachelard saw this electromagnetic collision as a "happening" in spacetime and asked, "what poet will furnish us with the metaphors for which this new language cries out?" Bachelard also suggested that "time acts through repetition more than through duration." I used to annotate my lab notebooks with poor drawings labeled "What I Saw": a bridge between the schematic drawings in our textbooks and the alien equipment we used in lab. In his *Atlas of Physiological Chemistry,* Otto Funke described his method of depicting what he saw in his microscope, so careful was he that he assured readers: "I have faithfully copied the shadows…" I find that wholly admirable, if also implausible.

SERENA RODRIGUEZ Often, when I set out to write a poem it is out of necessity, rather than desire. Like many of us who write from those difficult experiences that I/we so often tuck away within the depths of our bones, there is a bubbling over that happens, bringing us to the page. It might be a smell of certain soaps, or the way wind hits the cottonwoods just right, that brings me back to a place that needs to be recalled and excavated. The same goes for *"i had a form,"* which came in pieces through snippets of memory from the failure of my kidneys, the copious amounts of prednisone that carried me until it was "safe" to give birth to my child at 24 weeks, to the transplant that left my belly a scarred reminder of where I had been. As the fleeting thoughts came back, the poem came into being—the shifts mirror the chaotic hospital moments, of regret, quietude mixed with clusters of noise, childhood and hunger, for both my grandmother's love and the daydreams and damaging assumptions of motherhood so many of us hold close to our identity.

NAYT RUNDQUIST My creative process has been greatly influenced by the experimental nature of flash. I've been fascinated by bending and breaking the "rules" of fiction. Eschewing traditional character, dialogue, and other elements has opened space to see how far I can push tone and mood, and atmosphere, especially within the frame of science fiction, fantasy, and horror concepts. My favorite works of fiction linger in the feelings evoked more than the plot or characters. Creative practice, for me, has also been about reconnecting with myself, loved ones, and writing friends. Helping fellow writers hash through story ideas, trading feedback, and commiserating over writer's block has rekindled several amazing friendships. I believe creating, at its core, is about human connection. *"Grasping for Hummingbirds"* came to me after several years of personal loss. It is about grief and the aftermath of miscarriage. Framing the experiences as a haunted house story and horror film allowed me to reflect on the events and to find a way to the other side of the pain.

BEATRICE SZYMKOWIAK *"Viscera," "Blades of Grass," "Of Be/coming"* are from my larger collection titled *B / RDS* which is part of an investigation into the new environmental trajectory of the Anthropocene, and our environmental responsibility. The project is focused on *The Birds of America*—J. J. Audubon's iconic ornithological and archival work. Knowing that North America has lost three billion birds since 1970 (*Science*, 2019) inspired a process of lyrical erasure and reflection, to question disconnected approach to nature and the impulse to archive nature. My writing process starts by considering the text of *Birds of America* (the *Ornithological Biography* accompanying the drawings) as an archival cage. This is why I resolved to strictly abide by the rule of keeping the order of the words from the text-source—my text source being the *Birds of America* in alphabetical order. I then selectively erase the textual cage to reveal its ambiguity and the complex relationship between humanity and nature. As the cage disappears, birds escape, their voices inextricably entangled with ours. The "we" becomes equivocal. Slashes sever words, like wings or bird-shot pellets, reminding us that we are at a crossroad, and that we have a responsibility for the future of our planet.

N'DEA TUCKER As a visual storyteller, I am most inspired by and inclined to write stories that interrogate perspective and reality. The dimensions that shape our experiences and the rules we've created for ourselves—how do these bend and warp to make life as we know it? As a black woman, I've known the world to favor telling or listening to stories from white and / or cis-male lenses. With time, I've realized one of many reasons for this is ease. Stories from white, cis, straight, male, able-bodied, etc. perspectives are unburdened by factors believed to limit the stories of those labeled as society's outsiders. However, any outsider knows that these extra factors make us hyper aware of our existence, social status, and the way our perspective is at odds with and ignored by the powerful. *"Boy"* and *"I Am the Dark Side of the Sun"* are abstract evocations of dissociation, becoming too cognizant of one's being and losing touch with the present. *"Quinta-VI"* is a story grounded in a reality we recognize, following a young woman of color seeking to understand her place in her world. I create works centered on society's outsiders, as our lives balance perpetually on the precipice of existential anxiety. I created *"Quinta-VI"* the summer of 2019 while reflecting on the twenty-teens, and I was further inspired by the events of 2020. In times marked by upheaval, modern art splits. While some seek to highlight real issues, mainstream media tends to favor easy distraction. Many choose to glorify the past and smother the present to simplify the future, continuing cycles of despair, snowballing old lies into new problems. The same themes haunt the Rosaecea Galaxy in *"Quinta-VI."* Quinta is burdened by the guilt of a past she cannot recall. Though her palette is radiant, the grit of her world works in opposition. The aesthetic for *"Quinta-VI—Character Art"* featured on the back and front cover is loud and timeless, filled with bright shiny colors and a mix of retro styles. It references our real society's abuse of nostalgia, mimicking the glamorous facades of bygone eras—and much like ours, Quinta's world is far from glamorous. It is rotten with suffering and corruption, dying at an alarming rate, and no one in power seems to care. Quinta speaks to the eclectic and rebellious nature of today's youth—forced to reckon with a past by which they too feel overwhelmed, and forced to create a future they can hardly begin to imagine.

ERIC WEISKOTT I write poems directly into a word processor and then revise them painstakingly afterwards. The idea for ***"Body as Eschaton"*** came to me instantaneously. The conceit seemed encapsulated by the first two lines, which arrived already separated into two columns in my mind: *"Tree in lake, / body as eschaton."* I wanted to figure out how to make the syntax cross the boundary between the images. At first I kept writing sentences that spanned the two columns, but they muddied the images, which felt to me like they needed to remain separate. When I composed the list of objects for the body side I realized I could reuse it without reiterating it on the tree side using brackets. *"Body as Eschaton"* uses typographical space to orchestrate a duet between two images, a tree in a lagoon and your body seen, as if from the outside, as the limit of phenomenal existence. I'm not sure how exactly the two images harmonize except that the lagoon swallows the list of objects used to build your body.

JANE WILLIAMS My work is an instinctive visual journey into landscapes remembered from my intimate relationship with the natural world around me and the interior landscape of the heart which I access through states of stillness. I work intuitively laying down colour, taking away and adding repeatedly until the image reveals its potency in the depth and texture. The finished painting reads like a fairytale with a silent narrative of light embroidered with dark threads of anticipation which invite us to ask questions beyond our usual perceptions. In **"Somewhere in Between"** I strive to capture the lightness of being without the weight of ego *"Untethered"* is about relinquishing the sense of self to the ocean. And **"Tending the Sorrow"** attempts to depict our relentless need to protect and nurture those we love.

YU HSUAN WU I am a Taiwanese poet. For me, the duty of being a creator is not to create, but to receive, to give a perceivable and aesthetic form to the world that I receive. I believe that it is those symbols that trigger mental states that can capture the hazy and fleeting sense of existence. I will continue to explore and revise, to find expressive symbolic images and to embody poetry in my works. **"Stay Together"** is my understanding of emotional change, and a person's loyalty to his or her own emotional immutability.